Human Liberation
in a Feminist Perspective—A Theology

Published by The Westminster Press

Books by Letty M. Russell

Household of Freedom: Authority in Feminist Theology

Becoming Human *(Library of Living Faith)*

Growth in Partnership

The Future of Partnership

Human Liberation in a Feminist Perspective—A Theology

Christian Education in Mission

Books edited by Letty M. Russell

Feminist Interpretation of the Bible

The Liberating Word:
A Guide to Nonsexist Interpretation of the Bible

Human Liberation in a Feminist Perspective — A Theology

By LETTY M. RUSSELL

THE WESTMINSTER PRESS   1974
Philadelphia

Scripture quotations from the Revised Standard Version of the Bible are copyright, 1946 and 1952, by the
Division of Christian Education of the National Council
of Churches, and are used by permission.

BOOK DESIGN BY DOROTHY ALDEN SMITH

Published by The Westminster Press®
Philadelphia, Pennsylvania

PRINTED IN THE UNITED STATES OF AMERICA

9   8   7

Library of Congress Cataloging in Publication Data

Russell, Letty M.
  Human liberation in a feminist perspective.

  Includes bibliographical references.
  1. Freedom (Theology) 2. Salvation. 3. Woman (Theology) I. Title.
BT810.2.R87   261.8'34'12   74–10613
ISBN 0–664–24991–4

To my grandmother, Letty Mandeville Towl
my mother, Miriam Towl Russell
my niece, Letty Mandeville Berry
And to all the generations of sisters
they represent

CONTENTS

FOREWORD

Just as the *call for salvation* from transitoriness to attain immortality could be heard in every corner of the ancient world, today a *cry for liberation* is shouted by the oppressed, the humiliated, and the offended in this inhuman world.

In those early days the Christian church heard this call for salvation. People experienced saving power in Christ, in the proclamation of the gospel and in the Sacraments. With comprehensive intellectual integrity Christian theologians gave an account of the gospel message of salvation.

Will the Christian church hear the cry of liberation this time and suffer with those who suffer? Will men and women experience the compelling force of God's liberation "on earth as it is in heaven" in Christ, in the proclamation and in the powerful manifestation of the Holy Spirit? Will Christian theologians be able, this time, to account for "the hope that is in them"?

This seems to be the decisive question now, not only for Christians—so often of little faith—but also for humanity as a whole—which seems to have lost its sense of direction.

In our time, contributions to a comprehensive Christian Theology of Liberation have been forthcoming out of the most diverse quarters of misery in our fragmented world. For instance, James Cone wrote *Black Theology and Black Power* (1969). His "Black Theology" has roots in the experiences of suffering and struggle of the black slaves in the

United States. Gustavo Gutiérrez published *A Theology of Liberation* (1972) reflecting the experience and expectations of restless groups in the Latin-American churches. Frederick Herzog (1972) and Rosemary Ruether (1973) followed with liberation theologies. Herzog showed us the meaning of liberation in the light of the Gospel of John. Ruether confronted "human hope with Christian history and American power." It is almost impossible to keep track of the countless articles, conferences, and lectures on the same theme.

It is possible that *liberation theology* will become a new ecumenical point of convergence for the most different traditions, experiences, and struggles. One has the impression that it is here that hope is really accounted for in a practical and concrete way. Even more, one cannot get away from the impression that praxis becomes full of hope, and that diverse, concrete situations are turned into a point of departure for a common journey. Liberation begins in the specific situation of external and internal oppression. For that reason, liberation can never be conceived in general terms. The freedom one has set out to find is, however, a common realm. It is universal or it is not freedom at all.

Coming after the above-mentioned publications, Letty Russell Hoekendijk's book, HUMAN LIBERATION IN A FEMINIST PERSPECTIVE—A THEOLOGY, is the most profound contribution to a theology of human liberation. It is through and through a theological book. Not just a religious benediction of an already existing secular movement. Rather, the opposite is true. This book is a contribution to theology, written out of a specific involvement and a conscious engagement in the liberation of women: many years of pastoral experience with the poor, the blacks, and the Puerto Ricans in East Harlem; active participation in Christian women's movements and civil rights struggles. This book offers an exceedingly fortunate combination of theology and life; of Christian action and Biblical reflection. As is the case with Cone and Gutiérrez, it does not simply suggest another item on our theological agenda. It challenges us to do theology in a different style: to reflect critically and hopefully (solidly based on Biblical promises) on praxis. After all, the phony distinctions between "theory," as traditionally understood, and "praxis" do not lead us anywhere. The basic unity of Christian life and a wholistic approach to the Bible become significant in a new way. The dialectic of Bible work and liberation work in this book might lead us to ever-new surprises of insight and experience.

The "Feminist Perspective" never deteriorates into a partisan and one-sided frame of reference. This specific perspective simply indicates the *Sitz im Leben* out of which this contribution to liberation theology was written. Feministic objectives are never allowed to ruin the argument or to cloud over the purpose of this book.

Theology operating in an action-reflection model is concrete *charismatic theology,* that is, a style of doing theology within the context of the liberation of humankind. Precisely in this respect, it is a theology for the whole charismatic community of believers; *pro*—and not *contra*—other frontiers of hope where, in other configurations, people reach out for the freedom of Christ. It is delightful that in this feminist book the reader will be invited, even urged, to discover her or his own task and potential, in order to participate in God's all-embracing liberation movement, and to join in the action-reflection of her or his own specific situation.

Just as black theology has succeeded in making "white Christians" and theologians insecure in their traditional roles, so this feminist theology will deprive men of their masculine security. Black theology requests, even urges, nonblacks to get rid of their whiteness as an adequate mode of their existence, and, at last, risk being human-in-a-new-style. In the same fashion feminist theology requests and urges men to give up their male chauvinistic pride so that they may be set free to become fully human. In order to qualify as true liberation movements, *black liberation* from the oppressors and *women's liberation* from the traditionally fixed set of feminine roles should regard themselves as steps on the road toward a *human liberation of people,* becoming free in conformity with the authentic humanness of the Son of Man. The questioning of the role security of both "whites" and "males" should, therefore, be regarded as an opening up of their own specific possibilities, to reach out for a total and full humanness with others.

Letty Russell speaks about a "Journey Toward Freedom." No concrete liberation should be used to set up another oppressor with the roles reversed. Liberation does not mean fighting all the other members of the human family so that our specific group will be on top. Each one of the liberation movements opens a new front against the inhumanity of life. "Liberation is a journey with others, for others, toward God's future." In our concern for freedom, we are no longer allowed to be parochial. Rather, we are challenged to break down the always present ideological fixations of our own specific concerns. It is a matter of deep regret that, time and again, various liberation theologies fight each other in trying to define "the source of all evil." Socialists pontificate that capitalism is at the bottom of everything that went wrong. Racism and sexism are regarded as mere epiphenomena. Others point to racism as the root of all evil. In women's liberation, sexism is often considered to be the beginning of all humiliating oppression. Finally, ecologists could make a case by using what has happened in the exploitation of "voiceless" nature as a model of what one part of humankind has done to other members of the human family. This whole debate is, however, merely another manifestation of "bad metaphysics of evil"! To be sure, different movements set different priorities. In principle, however, no one liberation has a priority over other liberations. In all these specific movements, only the all-inclusive realm of freedom can have the first priority. Liberation of one particular group of people can be authentic only insofar as it includes freedom *for* the others, never *against* them.

The time may have come to divest ourselves of the ideological fixations of our own peculiar concerns and to seek concrete cooperation with other liberation movements. It is impossible to eliminate racism without putting an end to economic exploitation by one part of the human family of their brothers and sisters. True human rights for women is a utopia as long as we refuse to eliminate racism and a competitive society. It is great that this book by Letty Russell extends an open invitation and offers an unreserved readiness for cooperation to black, Latin-American, and sociocritical theologies, acknowledging how much it has learned from these movements.

The cry for freedom is universal. Ever since Paul related the groaning of the whole enslaved universe to the hope of Christians (Rom., ch. 8), authentic Christian universalism has been at home in this crying out for freedom. Once more, Paul expressed the Christian response in his jubilation about communion with Christ (Gal. 3:28): "There is neither Jew nor Greek, there is neither slave nor free, there is neither male nor female; for you are all one in Christ Jesus." Both these passages of Scripture, so often referred to in the following text, are the solid foundations of the Christian resurrection movement. These words ought to be translated into action today, in the church (how much does it need it!) and, simultaneously, in society (it has been waiting on tiptoe!). "For freedom Christ has set us free . . ." (Gal. 5:1), a freedom of the whole of life in the fullness of the Triune God.

This book "attempts great things, and hopes for great things." We cannot be content with less. Whoever decides to take to the road to freedom, as sketched in the following pages, will be in need of the perseverance of hope and the courage of faith. Life will not be less difficult, but it will become meaningful!

ELISABETH MOLTMANN-WENDEL
JÜRGEN MOLTMANN

Tübingen

INTRODUCTION

"Liberation Now!" is a constant slogan of our times. It is on the lips of countless women and men in every part of the globe. Whatever the language spoken, or the words used, the call for liberation is not just an empty slogan, but a *cri de coeur*. It is a cry from the heart; a cry out of oppression; a cry for a new future, beginning *now!*

As recently as 1970 women in the United States were united in singing "Liberation Now" as a theme song for their first national Liberation Day in commemoration of the Fiftieth Anniversary of the passing of the amendment that gave them the right to vote. The song affirmed that it was not "masculinity" nor "femininity," but "humanity that we both share." The text expressed a determination to work toward a new humanity in which women, men, and the whole world are free "to make love, not war."[1]

This ferment of freedom is not new, either to women or to other oppressed groups. The same echo, for instance, comes to us in the words of Raden Adjeng Kartini, a pioneer in the struggle for Indonesian independence and the liberation of her own sisters through educational reform. In 1899 she wrote:

In my thoughts and sympathies, I do not belong to the world of the Indies but to that of my white sisters who are fighting for progress in the distant west. . . . Century-old, unbreakable traditions hold us today in a relentless grip. One day that grip will slacken and we shall be able to struggle against it, but it will not be for a long, a very long time. It will come about, I am sure, but perhaps not for another three or four generations. Oh, you cannot imagine what it is to love the new age with all one's heart and soul, yet to be bound hand and foot, chained to the laws and customs of our country. All our institutions are totally opposed to the progress for which I long in the interests of our people.[2]

Nor is freedom a new theme for Christian theology. The gospel is a message of liberation in Jesus Christ. It is good news to all people in every situation. Concretely, and in every place of external or internal oppression, liberation has arrived in the form of One sent as the bringer of a new humanity.

Yet today, in a world of revolutionary change, the freedom chorus is constantly growing in a symphony of the groaning of creation. It is heard, not only in the streets of San Diego, Harlem, or Prague, but also along the boulevards of Rio de Janeiro, Djakarta, or Johannesburg. It is even echoed in our own hearts. We all wish we knew how it would feel to be free! We all are beginning to sense a restlessness in our bones as we try to take steps toward liberation *now,* liberation for others and for ourselves.

These are especially exciting and challenging times for women. Exciting, because so many new ideas, life-styles, and ways of service are opening up. Challenging, because women are often moving away from old securities along new paths where there are many questions and few answers. Every field of learning, every skill, every life-style, becomes a new arena of experiment as women seek out their own perspectives, the contribution that they would make in building a new house of freedom.

Certainly, theology is no exception to this excitement and challenge. Women are voicing their search for liberation by rejecting oppressive and sexist religious traditions that declare that they are socially, ecclesiastically, and personally inferior because of their sex. They are digging deeper into their traditions, raising questions about the authority of the church "fathers," and searching out the hidden evidence of the contributions of the church "mothers" to the life and mission of the church. They are looking for truly authentic and liberating roots as they search for a *usable past.* At the same time, women are joining other oppressed groups in seeking out a clear vision of a new society of justice and *shalom,* so that they can join the global struggle for a *usable future.*[3]

These women are *feminists* because they advocate changes that will establish political, economic, and social equality of the sexes.[4] In a Christian context they reflect on the way in which theology can become more complete, as all people are encouraged to contribute to the meaning of faith from their own perspective. Such action and theory form the basis of *feminist theology.* It is "feminist" because the women involved are actively engaged in advocating the equality and partnership of women and men in church and society.

It is not *feminine theology* because femininity refers to a culturally defined set of roles and personal characteristics that elaborate the biological ability of women to bear children. According to the stereotypes of Western culture, some theology is masculine and some is feminine. One theology might contain elements of aggression, assertion, and analytical thinking; another might have elements of wholistic and contextual sensitivity and a concern for interrelationships of persons and of human nurture. But, as Mary Daly has stated, all theology must be "concerned with the problems of persons in relation to others" and not with preconceived notions about the nature of women around which an isolated theology is developed.[5] For this reason feminist theology strives to be *human* and not just *feminine,* as other forms of theology should strive to be *human* and not just *masculine.*

Feminist theology today is, by definition, *liberation theology* because it is concerned with the liberation of all people to become full participants in human society.[6] *Liberation theology is an attempt to reflect upon the experience of oppression and our actions for the new creation of a more humane society.* In the words of Gustavo Gutiérrez, a Latin-American theologian:

Theology of liberation attempts to reflect on the experience and meaning of faith based on the commitment to abolish injustice and to build a new society; this theology must be verified by the practice of that commitment, by active, effective participation in the struggle which the exploited classes have undertaken against their oppressors.[7]

This perspective on theology is an elaboration of *political theology* or *theology of hope* as seen in such writers as Jürgen Moltmann and Johannes Metz.[8] According to Moltmann, Christian political theology is an attempt to relate the eschatological message of freedom to sociopolitical reality. The focus of Christian hope is not simply on the open future but on the future of the hopeless.[9]

Feminist theology has common roots with many types of, so-called, Third World liberation theologies. *Third World* is used here to refer to people living outside the United States and Western Europe *(First World)*, and of the Communist bloc countries in Eastern Europe *(Second World)*, and includes their descendants living in racial oppression in any country. Third World has economic as well as racial overtones pointing toward experiences of economic exploitation and colonialism. The term is presently used by groups in North America as a way of emphasizing that nonwhite groups are a majority of the world's population. They make up two thirds of the world's population, although they are a minority among those who hold political, social, and economic power. Women belong to all these various "worlds," and as such they are numbered among the oppressed and oppressors. Yet in relation to the male domination of the social structures of most societies women have a growing consciousness of their own oppression. In speaking of themselves as an oppressed world majority some women have adopted the term *Fourth World*. In this sense, Barbara Burris writes: "We identify with all women of all races, classes, and countries all over the world. The female culture is the Fourth World."[10]

Like Third World liberation theology, feminist theology is written out of an experience of oppression in society. It interprets the search for salvation as a journey toward freedom, as a process of self-liberation in community with others in the light of hope in God's promise. Together with other people searching for freedom, women wish to speak of the hope that is in them. They want to tell the world that they are part of God's plan of human liberation.

This book comes out of my own experience in the search for liberation. Its very shape represents the constant process of action-reflection which has led me in a journey with others, for others, toward God's future. Some of its themes grow out of that journey. The concern for the meaning of God's action in situations of oppression was a matter of constant search in my work for fifteen years in an ecumenical parish of a black and Puerto Rican community in New York City. The world perspective on human liberation was nurtured through work on behalf of renewal of the life and mission of the church in the World Council of Churches, as I participated in the studies on the Missionary Structure of the Congregation; Christians Within Changing Institutions; and Sexism in the 1970's. Concern for sisterhood in the context of the thrust for the elimination of racism has been sharpened in working with the National Board of the YWCA of the United States and with the YWCA of India. Commitment to the unity of the church has been constantly tested by teaching and working in Roman Catholic as well as Protestant colleges and seminaries and communities in the United States and abroad.

The text is not a finished product. It is part of the journey toward freedom which I have shared with my sisters and brothers in many places. In my effort to contribute my own perspective to that of many others who would interpret the meaning of the good news in today's world, I have simply tried to set down a few notes on aspects of the gospel of liberation which is my basis of hope. The notes at the back of the book are a sign of this collective journey and provide resources for those who wish to examine any particular "road" in more detail. The dedication to the generations of important women in my own life is a symbol of my conviction that *all* sisters are important in the search for a new humanity.

In an attempt to use nonsexist language I have not only refrained from using the word *he* for God, who is beyond sexual distinctions, but also used pronouns that refer either to both men and women or to the specific human grouping under discussion. The reader will notice that many quotations have inserted or changed words in brackets. This serves two purposes. It reminds everyone of the pervasive use of male pronouns in the generic sense in the English language. It also brings the quotations into line with the intended language practices of this book. Those men who feel excluded by the frequent use of female pronouns and references to women should remember that at this moment in history a feminist perspective is needed which seeks to emphasize the inclusion of women in the search for theological, social, political, and economic equality. Language reflects our patterns of thought and action. That a change in language usage is not as difficult as some people claim is indicated in this book where awkward language constructions are *preferred* to acting as if women are the "invisible part of the human race." The problem of *usable language* is discussed in more detail in Chapter 3.

The reader will also notice that certain themes such as *human liberation* and *servanthood* recur in the various chapters. This style of writing in a spiral that constantly returns to basic themes and holds them up to look at them from the angle of new evidence and perspective is part of the action-reflection process. Basic themes and motifs come to the fore no matter what theological aspect is being investigated, but each time it is hoped that new insights are added. This is especially true of *service, diakonia,* or *ministry*. This concept pervades the Biblical references to God, Jesus Christ, and his followers. Attention is focused on *diakonia* because liberation theology must come to grips with the way in which it can be interpreted as a scandal of the gospel, but not necessarily as a scandal of the oppressed who have been led to reject servanthood because of its overtones of subordination. Further discussion of this problem is found in Chapter 5.

The investigation of HUMAN LIBERATION IN A FEMINIST PERSPECTIVE begins with an overview of the *Journey Toward Freedom*. In a sense, it begins where it ends, with the vision that impels us toward liberation now! The middle part explores the common themes of *Human Liberation and Theology* and the ways in which we can *Search for a Usable Past* which will give us an adequate basis for a usable human future. The latter part takes up three themes of human liberation and examines them in the light of Christian tradition. Each chapter—*Salvation and Conscientization; Incarnation and Humanization; Communion in Dialogue*—is a praxis of freedom. Each one is an attempt to reflect theologically, and therefore Biblically, on some of the ways liberation is experienced in the lives of Third World and Fourth World people. The end is a *Prologue,* an invitation to each of us, including myself, to make a new beginning on the ongoing revolution of freedom which is part of God's plan for the whole human race.

Human Liberation
in a Feminist Perspective—A Theology

1: JOURNEY
   TOWARD FREEDOM

Freedom is a journey with others and for others toward God's future. Freedom can never be defined once and for all. Freedom defined is freedom no longer, because it always transcends all our definitions or concepts. It can be experienced and celebrated only as it breaks into our lives as new awareness of hope in God's future, and new confidence in the growing ability to experience and share love with others.

When we try to describe freedom in our lives as women and men in a world and church in change, we usually turn to the word "liberation." This is not because we can be any more specific about what it means, but because liberation helps us to focus on a *process* of struggle with ourselves and others toward a more open future for humanity. As we experiment with what freedom might mean, we discover that the struggle toward liberation varies with each person and with each human community.

If someone were to ask a woman *what freedom means for her*, she might answer the question with one of a variety of possible descriptions, depending on her situation and the influence of particular revolutions of freedom in which she is immediately involved. If she were a middle-class woman in the United States, she might simply list the present goals of the women's liberation groups which make up the organized part of the movement: freedom from exploitation in the *labor market,* equal pay and employment practices, and quality child care for working women; freedom to develop more meaningful and creative styles of *family life* so that the woman is not left to living vicariously through her husband and children and is not trapped by domestic isolation from the public sphere and by enforced triviality in the thirty years of her life which remain after her children are fully grown; freedom from *sexual exploitation,* and degrading use of her body for entertainment and advertising promotion.[1]

If she were a Third World woman in the United States, she might list freedom from her position of double disadvantage brought about by racism and sexism, asserting that "human rights are indivisible."[2] Or if she were a woman in India, she might list her goals in terms of freedom from arranged marriages, sufficient food to eat, a job for her husband, or education for her children. A woman in one of the African Portuguese colonies or South Africa might put freedom from white colonialism and intentional practices of genocide at the top of her list. And so the lists could go, on and on, in every part of the globe.

A woman might prefer to answer the question of what freedom means by simply saying she wants freedom to be herself and to be accepted as herself, a whole human being. Or she might even refer to the incomplete and ever-changing process of liberation itself by saying that she will not know what her freedom means until she obtains a small piece of it and can describe it, at the same time looking toward the next possibility of freedom that begins to show itself over the horizon. For the promises of liberation, like the promises of God, are not fully known except as they are experienced, and then they always have an "overspill" of longing that points to the next fulfillment.[3]

This *situation variability* of liberation means that in every situation, every culture, every subculture, the things *from* which people would be free and the things *for* which they long are different. For every woman who longs to be free from the drudgery and boredom of her home, there is another woman who longs to be free from the drudgery and boredom of a job that keeps her out of the home, and another who wishes she has a home or a job!

So how can we talk of human freedom in a global perspective? Definitions and blueprints are out, and even situational descriptions can never even begin to do the job. Perhaps the only way is by sharing clues and stories of liberation which can help each of us to search out our own road toward the future which God holds open for us. Or perhaps by sharing our common longing and speaking in poetry and visions. In the words of the haunting jazz melody of Billy Taylor, each of us somewhere deep in our heart sings, "I wish I knew how it would feel to be free!" Out of the experience of black oppression the song cries out, "I wish I could break all these chains holding me . . . say all the things I should say . . . for the whole world to hear!"[4]

One way for us to begin as Christians is to return to another haunting description of the journey toward freedom which we find in Rom. 8:14–27. Remembering the Biblical story of liberation in the exodus and the resurrection, we can look together at how *groaning for freedom, discovery of freedom,* and *horizon of freedom* appear to be happening in the experience of women in today's world.

GROANING FOR FREEDOM

In Paul's description of the struggle toward liberation the first thing that strikes us is his vivid picture of the whole universe groaning for freedom. In Rom. 8:22–23 Paul tells us:

As we all know, up to the present time, the creation in all its parts groans with pain like the pain of childbirth. But not just creation alone groans; we ourselves, although we have tasted already the *apéritif* of the Spirit, we groan inwardly because we are still anticipating our adoption as children and the full liberation of our human existence.[5]

Solidarity of Groaning. What a relief! We discover that there is a solidarity of groaning. We are not the only ones who feel trapped and frustrated. Our sisters and brothers, even our environment, share together in the oppressive structures of society. Paul explains, by reference to the Fall in which all nature was subject to dislocation because of human disobedience, that "the script of our frustration" has a very long history.[6] In its state of mortality and decadence all the universe longs for the fulfillment of God's new creation when all the parts will be born again in harmony, when the New Age promised by God and begun in Jesus Christ will be fulfilled.

We also discover as Christians that we are not saved *out of* this groaning world, but as *part of* it. We are saved in hope which comes from having already tasted of the firstfruits of the Spirit of freedom (the *apéritif*). Insofar as we have a small foretaste of God's gift of freedom, we are also led to see more clearly that this gift is intended by God for all women and men.[7] Our heightened restlessness and longing, brought about by this foretaste, can only direct us toward participating in God's solidarity with humankind. It thrusts us to join with Christ, who "emptied himself, taking the form of a servant," in order to be part of this journey with others and for others toward God's future (Phil. 2:7).

Oppression of Women. The women's liberation movement in the United States and other nations helps to underline this experience of solidarity in groaning. Through a steady flow of documents, papers, stories, and actions, women testify that they have discovered that male domination and the submission of women is a sign of personal and social groaning.[8] This is brought about, according to the feminist perspective, not by God's original design for creation, but by human disobedience and dislocation.

Certainly this experience of oppression does not always involve the *classic forms* of political, economic, and racial oppression because women tend to share the social status of their husbands. Where men have had access to the goods of life, women have not been bred to inferiority because they were destined to be the mothers of the next generation of sons. Women elites in every society have shared the social advantages of their class, and participated in the oppression of the other classes. Yet at the same time women have been culturally "programmed" to accept a life of subservience to father and husband. Frequently they have been denied access to the education and self-development that would make them capable of strengthening the self-development of their children and participating in public sectors of human life.

Domination of women by men is an ancient and persistent form of the subjection of one human being to a permanent status of inferiority because of sex. The famous quote of August Bebel in declaring that the changes of history can be marked according to the progress of women may not be completely accurate historically.[9] Yet it expresses the not so accidental analogy between sexism, racism, and all forms of economic exploitation. "Woman was the first human being to come into bondage: she was a slave before the male slave existed."[10] The oppression of women is the most universal form of exploitation which supports and perpetuates the other forms of exploitation in both church and society.[11]

As Jürgen Moltmann has pointed out, there have been a whole succession of freedom movements that have expressed the human striving for liberation in Western society. Each new movement has continued the gains of previous ones and has attempted to overcome the continuing disappointments. But "so far, no one of them has brought about the 'realm of freedom' itself, but each one has opened a new front in the struggle for freedom."[12]

In our present world the rising expectations of many oppressed peoples has led them to participate in their own movements toward liberation. Women belong to one of the groups who find that the liberties gained have not been adequate. As an oppressed majority they seek to break the peculiar chains of sexism which bind us all, both women and men. Aware of their solidarity with others in groaning, they want to add their own contribution to the revolutions of freedom.

Where some women have tasted the firstfruits of liberation they are even more persistent in declaring that token forms of equality are not sufficient. The taste of freedom leads them to join others who have tasted this "heady wine." They have joined the procession of their sisters in every age, in demanding freedom *from* dehumanizing social structures, in order that they might become free *for* participation in the social, political, and economic struggles for humanization which are taking place in our global society.

Freedom to Serve. For Christian women the experience of new freedom leads to new responsibility. Not only does the *apéritif* bring the "Spirit of freedom," but also it brings with it a commission *(oikonomia)* to act in ministry and service to the world with which they groan (II Cor. 3:17; 1:22). *They are being set free for service to others.* But what form should this service *(diakonia)* take? How can they use their new experience of groaning and longing to be free to work out better ways of expressing their solidarity with others?

The service of Christ is a calling to be instruments of God's help, not a calling to be subservient. Yet it is clearly also a calling to solidarity in working with others, and not to superiority. Solidarity in groaning and working with others to gain freedom to shape their future cannot be a form of dominance or manipulation. For, as many women now know from their own experience, service that perpetuates dependency is not service at all.

Voices from the Third World are clearly expressing this conviction when they distinguish between *micro-charity* and *macro-charity*.[13] In a technological society the problem of charity has changed. In a pretechnological era, only micro-charity was possible in which people expressed love for their immediate neighbor through gestures such as almsgiving, or individual forgiveness. In a technological society, on the other hand, all parts of the globe are linked together in impersonal structures of violence and injustice. In this situation it is macro-charity that addresses itself to liberation and justice for peoples caught in complex structures and human relationships which dehumanize their lives. The ethical issues become ones of global peace, development, nation-building, technological exploitation, and not just ways of helping our immediate neighbor in one community or nation.

Actually, of course, this is not new. There were always social as well as personal problems. There was always a need to work in solidarity with others on behalf of justice rather than in extending bits of charity. But now the question of how to carry out our work of *diakonia* has become urgent in the church and the world. It is urgent (1) because of the new hope of liberation and its social implications which have infected the hearts and minds of many people; (2) because of the demands of others that they find their *own* journey to freedom and shake off the shackles of dependency; and (3) because the credibility of the church stands and falls with its response to the groaning peoples of the world. Gutiérrez emphasizes this point in saying:

... the question regarding the theological meaning of liberation is, in truth, a question *about the very meaning of the Church.* ... Today the seriousness and scope of the process which we call liberation is such that the Christian faith and the Church are being radically challenged. They are being asked to show what significance they have for the human task which has reached adulthood.[14]

Diakonia (service or ministry) has traditionally taken three forms.[15] *Curative diakonia* is the healing of the wounds of those who have become victims of life; providing help to the sick, the hungry, and the homeless. *Preventive diakonia* is attempting to curtail developments that might easily lead to restriction of full freedom for life; working through social action to provide vocational training centers, drug prevention programs, etc. *Prospective diakonia* is attempting to open the situation for a future realization of life; helping those who are outcasts from the dominant culture or society to participate fully in society or to reshape that society.

Until recently the church has specialized in curative or "Band-Aid" tasks, and women have strongly supported these causes. Gradually they have begun to realize that *diakonia* is genuine solidarity in groaning only when it moves toward preventive programs and finally into prospective advocacy of the rights of people to decide for themselves how to work out their political and social liberation. Prospective *diakonia* is what people want for themselves. The basic necessities of life, without a way to help in shaping life, do not necessarily lead to liberation. This means that serving young people, or the aged, or ghetto residents, or Third World and Fourth World people begins with *their participation* in setting the agenda, and picking the battles. As Paulo Freire writes:

This is why there can be no socio-economic development in a dual, "reflex," invaded society. For development to occur it is necessary: (a) that there be a movement of search and creativity having its seat of decision in the researcher; (b) that this movement occur not only in space, but in the existential time of the conscious searcher.[16]

Diakonia is a mutual action of people and not a giving of "things" to "things." This means a genuine struggle to see that the church takes steps to support prospective action on the part of those groups and movements working for their own liberation and development. Curative and preventive *diakonia* is always needed in the desperate situations of poverty, famine, and human psychological and physical damage or destruction, but it is not enough. Those who themselves have experienced a groaning and longing to be free must face up to the risky business of advocating human liberation in the process of working out better ways for expressing solidarity with others.

DISCOVERY OF FREEDOM

If we return to Paul's story of the journey toward freedom, we notice a striking description of the discovery of freedom. In Rom. 8:18–19 he tells us:

I consider that whatever we suffer now cannot be compared to all the splendour as yet not revealed, which is in store for us. The created universe is waiting on tiptoe for the children of God, to show what they are. In fact, the fondest dream of the universe is to catch a glimpse of real live children of God.

Children of God. In his poetic image we find that everyone who is working and longing for freedom is eagerly longing ("waiting on tiptoe") to catch a vision of what "it means to be free." For to be set free is to become real live children of God and to be part of a universe inhabited by these real live children!

Because we are all on this journey toward freedom together, we do not know exactly what children of God look like. Certainly if the members of Christian churches are presumed to represent them in any finished character, there is little to be expected! Christians seem to find themselves in a *minus situation* in this regard.[17] Just because they have received a foretaste of the Spirit, they realize how far they and others before them have fallen short of Paul's vision of living a life in Christ in which "there is neither Jew nor Greek, there is neither slave nor free, there is neither male nor female" (Gal. 3:23–29). This foretaste of the Spirit has also made them more conscious of the fact that *diakonia* involves being "less than others," submitting their plans to the plans of others they serve and to God.

At the same time they are called to live in a situation of groaning and longing in which the hope comes not from foolproof plans or illusions, doctrines or traditions, mythologies or ideologies, but from confidence in God's promise of liberation. This hope is in something we cannot see and something we cannot verify until it happens (Rom. 8:24–25). The new creation which God brings as the *adventus* or coming future is so *new* that it will be fully understood only in the light of the fulfillment of the resurrection.[18]

But in spite of this minus situation in the light of past and present failures and unfulfilled future promises, we have received the gift of the Spirit which sets us free to live without security and aids us in our weakness and inadequacy.[19]

Now then: In the same way the Spirit also comes to help us, weak that we are. We do not even know how to pray properly. The Spirit has to do the job for us, expressing our pleas in a way that could never be put into words. And God who X-rays our hearts, understands what the Spirit means in praying for God's own people in God's own way. (Rom. 8:26–27.)

The main clue that we have as Christians beyond this foretaste which both judges and comforts us is that of Jesus of Nazareth. In him we trust that God has made known the beginnings of the love, obedience, and true humanity which is the destiny of a restored creation. For women and men alike, Jesus embodies in his life, death, and resurrection what a truly human being *(anthrōpos)* might be like. One who would love and live and suffer for love of God and for others. He was not just a male *(anēr)*; he was for us *all*, a real live child of God! He was the second humanity (Adam) and showed both parts of humanity, male and female, both the cost and promise of freedom (I Cor. 15:45).[20] Dorothy Sayre describes the relation of Jesus and women in saying:

Perhaps it is no wonder that women were first at the Cradle and last at the Cross. They had never known a man like this Man—there never has been such another. A prophet and teacher who never nagged at them, never flattered or coaxed or patronized. . . . There is no act, no sermon, no parable in the whole Gospel that borrows its pungency from female perversity; nobody could possibly guess from the words and deeds of Jesus that there was anything "funny" about woman's nature.[21]

In searching out how the life-style of this One child of God applies to our own life-style and journey toward freedom, we can know that there are no easy answers. After all, the cross was not an easy road to take toward freedom! Yet the Spirit of Christ does help us in our weakness and can give us "the ability to distinguish between spirits" (*diakrisis*, I Cor. 12: 10). With the inspiration of the Spirit we can seek out the signs of the times in a critical manner and find where our calling to action lies.

Ferment of Freedom. One of the places to search is in the women's liberation movement and in other liberation movements. For the presence of the "ferment of freedom" among them certainly puts this question with ever-new urgency. What do real live children of God look like? What does it mean to be human? In spite of the gospel of liberation and the words and actions of Jesus, the church has too long supported the idea that nonwhites, non-Westerners, and non-males are slightly less than human. They contribute little to "real culture" and need to look up to the dominant political and ecclesiastical hierarchies to find out how they ought to act and think.

To free oneself from patriarchalism, colonialism, and imperialism it is necessary to discover that all human beings have a culture. All are capable of thinking about and interpreting their world and shaping their own histories with the tools at their disposal. In describing his work with peasants in Brazil, Freire writes that illiterates needed first to discover that they were *subjects* "in the world and with the world" and not just objects to be manipulated by fate and unseen powers.

From that point of departure, the illiterate would begin to effect a change in his [or her] former attitudes, by discovering himself [or herself] to be a maker of the world of culture, by discovery that he [or she], as well as the literate person, has a creative and re-creative impulse.[22]

Too long the myths about *class* have been used as self-fulfilling prophecy. Just because a group of people have a common expectancy of life opportunities represented by their economic capabilities in the labor and commodity market, this is no reason to accept the idea that those with less economic worth or potential in a particular economic system are, therefore, inferior human beings. The proletariat may have "nothing but their children," but the elites of society are also made less human by the structures of domination, exploitation, and dehumanization which they perpetuate.

The same type of myths have been used to enslave millions of people in demonic *caste* systems. These castes operate not only in certain religious traditions such as that of the Hindus in India, but also in modern systems of *racism* and *sexism*. Max Weber tells us that along with class that functions in the economic order, social status is a constantly interlocking factor in the social order of society. When this status or honor is fixed so that certain groups are placed in a closed caste (from which there is no exit), they become outcasts with permanent social inferiority.[23]

This is what has happened to Third World people in the United States, who are not just separate ethnic groups, but "inferior human beings" with low status. The same dynamics are operative in relation to women who, by birth, find themselves as a separate and inferior caste in relation to male social norms and privilege. Caste is often even more insidious and dehumanizing than class because it is almost impossible to overcome one's sex or the color of one's skin. The only way to break through such a web of oppression is to insist not only on economic equality but also on full human equality and honor in society.

On every continent, but especially in North America, much has been made of the competition between the liberation movements mainly devoted to the elimination of racism, and those mainly devoted to the elimination of sexism. Two things are obvious about this discussion from the outset. One is, that as long as the most outspoken opponents of sexism represent white, middle-class women, the women who are committed first of all to the freedom of their own people, in whatever country or community, are right to be suspicious about the motives and results of such a movement. In this regard, Valerie Russell writes:

I am not saying that white women do not have a new vision which is non-oppressive, but it must be defined and demonstrated to be believed. Trust must be earned. *How such trust is earned should be a major focus* for any women's group seeking to deal with questions of liberation. . . . In their historical eye, the white woman has been their enemy. It is now necessary for white women to prove that just as they will no longer play the pampered, soft, sex-object role, they will also no longer play the role of being the enemy of their Third World sisters.[24]

The other clear issue is that *all women* have so much in common, that the best tactic of the preservers of the status quo is to make sure that they convince different groups of women that they have nothing in common. This will prevent the use of their collective power for the elimination of racism, sexism, and classism in the building of a more humane society.

Black women are certainly divided on the issue of their role in the feminist movement. Many want to have nothing to do with this white women's affair. Yet, as seen in the formation of the National Black Feminist Organization in 1973, there is a growing awareness of the need for black women to struggle against the "double jeopardy" of their race and sex that places them at the bottom of the economic and social ladder. Black women are becoming aware of the false myth that they should follow their men and become dependent and supportive. Some perceive it as a black male way of buying into the white male's image of the female role. They are determined to keep and develop their own self-reliance, forged in the fires of slavery and oppression, so that it can be employed on behalf of black liberation and strengthened by solidarity with women of all races and cultures who struggle against oppression.[25]

Development of critical awareness among the women in the Fourth World regarding the divergence of race, culture, language, ideology, and tactics of groups working at different points to eliminate the web of oppression is essential in the struggle toward liberation. The struggle begins with woman in her own heart, mind, and actions as she learns to be *pro-woman*. But it must stretch around the world to all people (men, women, and children) who are looking for the freedom to shape their own futures and participate in the search for what it means to be children of God. Shirley Chisholm underlines this point in saying:

You must start in your own homes, your own schools and your own churches. . . . I don't want you to go home and talk about integrated schools, churches, or marriages when the kind of integration you are talking about is black and white. I ask you to work for—fight for—the integration of male and female, human and human. Franz Fanon pointed out in *Black Skins —White Masks* that the anti-Semite was eventually the antifeminist. And even further I want to indicate that all discrimination is eventually the same thing—antihumanism. That is my charge to you whether you are male or female.[26]

Critical Discernment. Women in the church are called to share this critical process of discerning what it means to be human and trying to live out their discoveries of freedom. The ability to discern the signs of the time and thus be able to work toward freedom is a gift of the Holy Spirit. The word that Paul uses here for discernment is *diakrisis* (I Cor. 12: 10).[27]

The function of *diakrisis* can help women and the church to take a prophetic stance over against society as they seek to discern God's actions and to *criticize* those parts of the world (including themselves) which deny God's plan and purpose of justice, freedom, and peace for humanity. In this way they can join others in helping to shape society and discovering new freedom, rather than being shaped by society and old cultural assumptions that close off the future.

In the past the church has frequently played roles or functions assigned to it by society. The church served the function of *public cult* in the Western Middle Ages, providing the heavenly "connections" for Christendom.[28] With the breakdown of Christendom in modern society it has been called to provide a *private cult*, serving the needs of the individual in industrial society in his or her private, religious sphere. In a world more and more becoming "post-religious" and not necessarily searching for its security in the sacred realm, such functions may become less necessary to society. This sets the church free to be itself over against the society, when this is necessary in the service of Christ and God's Mission in the world.

The *diacritical* role of discernment and critique is difficult to everyone, and especially for women who have been enculturated to spend time making people "like them." To begin with, it means having courage to be a *misfit* in society; acting and thinking with those who are groaning for liberation and working to disturb the status quo. The cost of this may mean becoming "marginal persons," those who don't fit with their peers or into accepted norms in either church or society.

Secondly, this type of Christian responsibility and critical awareness about the political and social realities of the world demands both *theological discernment* and a wide variety of *technical know-how.* This of course means that women will have to *do their homework* and be willing to take concrete actions for social change based on their *own* new consciousness of the social and theological issues at stake. For Christian women in this situation "doing theology" is not just an added luxury after developing expertise in other disciplines. Doing theology is itself an act of freedom! It is a critical means of searching out the right questions about the Bible and ecclesial tradition, about God and faith. Instead of accepting a certain text *(lectio)* delivered from the "fathers," serious questions *(quaestio)* must be raised in order to try to discern what it means to be real live children of God.

In the past, churchwomen's groups and organizations have had to settle for the supportive and listening role in matters of theological and social research and leadership in the church. *Now* it is time to play the listening role of Mary; listening to *Jesus* and acting out the gospel of freedom, rather than remaining in the church kitchen with Martha (Luke 10:38–42). Where women's groups find that they cannot move away from sewing, bazaars, and occasional Bible study, toward new forms of *diakonia* and serious theological and social reflection, they may no longer be able to serve the cause of human liberation. The frequent result of this passive type of marginal role by such groups is that they fail to attract the very type of serious and committed women who are needed in this struggle. It may be that in such a circumstance new structures and organizations for women need to be set up in which they find ways to support one another in *diakrisis* (critical and prophetic action).

Meeting together as women is not enough. Even mutual consciousness-raising and discussion of problems is not adequate. The liberation process is a continued struggle to act together with others to transform society by any means necessary. In such a risky undertaking of *diakrisis* the constant help of the Holy Spirit is a necessity. But that Spirit will not make the way easy. In the words of the poet Julius Lester, our prayer is not just for a critical consciousness, but also for the constant disturbing power which can cut that consciousness like a *razor*, disturbing us, and forcing us to prophetic action.[29] Thus we pray,

O God,
RAZE my consciousness. Amen.

HORIZON OF FREEDOM

If we return once again to Paul's description of the journey toward freedom, we become aware that we live constantly within a horizon of freedom. In Rom. 8:20 he says:

The creation is in the grip of frustration and futility. Not by its own choice. God made it so, and, therefore, there is always hope that one day the universe will be set free from the shackles of mortality and decadence and share the glorious freedom of the children of God.

Hope in God's Future. The horizon of freedom is hope! Hope is the expectation of faith that God's promised future will become a reality.[30] This "hope is not the opium of the people, but an impulse to change the world in the perspective of God's promises."[31]

The situation variability of liberation leads to a constant shifting of our horizon of freedom. We might hope for liberation as freedom from outside coercion and causation, or for a spontaneous affirmation of selfhood. At another time our hope might be for freedom as an alternative possibility for change or for freedom of choice and freedom to act on that choice. Yet our human hopes as Christians are always based on the perfect freedom of God. It is God's perfect freedom which is exercised in *being for us.* According to Moltmann, "God is not our utopia, but we are God's utopia. We are hoping because God hopes for us."[32] The Christ event initiates our freedom in such a way that we are drawn with all creation into the horizon of God's freedom by participating in the action of God on behalf of human liberation. Rubem Alves describes the horizon of freedom in saying:

The cross, then, which is fundamentally the symbol of the hopelessness and futurelessness that order and religion created, came to be seen as the beginning of a new possibility for history. If God suffers with and for . . . [us, we are] assured that God's personal negation of the negative in history is not a lonely voice. . . . Because . . . [God] suffers with and negates the unfreedom of today, it is possible to hope for a tomorrow in which . . . [we] will be made free.[33]

The nature of a horizon is that it always disappears and a new one appears as we move toward it. The horizon of freedom constantly changes and looks different as we journey with others and for others toward God's future. Because of the problems and difficulties and plain mess of the world in which we live, there appears to be no hope. The horizon closes in and there is no vision. Often our best planning and efforts bring little change in the immense problems of our world and the great problems of our lives.

In this case the future which we plan is always a problem. It is the *futurum* which we extrapolate out of the continued groaning of a world in pain.[34] The question we ask along with planners and futurists is, "*When* will justice, freedom, peace and dignity happen *if* they happen at all?" Yet for Christians this is not the last question. There is also always the future *(adventus)* which comes toward us from God as a *promise.* In relation to the *adventus* our question is not, "*When* will it happen, *if* ever," but, "How can we live *now as if* the horizon of that future has already broken into our lives through the Spirit of Jesus Christ?" The discovery of this new horizon of freedom leads us to actions because God hopes for us, and it is up to us to live *now as if* the "form of this world is passing away" and the new creation is already present in our lives (I Cor. 7:25–31).[35]

Already on Their Way. The women's liberation movement illustrates some of the fundamental facts of the *already . . . but not yet* character of liberation. By their new thoughts and actions women are saying that they are *already on their way* toward freedom. They know, however, that they have *not yet arrived* because no one is free until all are free. The horizon changes but does not disappear because a few people gain new privileges and responsibilities.

The stress on sisterhood stands as a constant reminder to women of the continuing responsibility for their other sisters and brothers in the world. Whatever gains women have made, they are only partial unless society and culture is restructured so that others have the same equal access to these changes, be they economic, political, social, or private. Those who have "made it," however they have made it, are coming to see that they have a responsibility to share the task of building new life-styles and a new society with all women and men and not just for themselves. Dana Densmore says to her sisters: "We are all one. All the same influences have acted upon us. If you have somehow escaped the consequences of your conditioning you are lucky, not superior, not different. We are all sisters."[36]

Another perspective which women's liberation movements help to underline concerning the character of all liberation movements is that *they are not the cause of disruption* in our societies. The many myths that blame women for disrupting families, discrediting motherhood, defeating the "real revolutions" of the radical left, and promoting juvenile delinquency are projections of those who would like to preserve the status quo. Just as blacks did not cause the disruptions flowing from racism in society, women did not cause the disruptions which flow from sexism. They are responding to the results of oppression and dislocation that are already all around us and trying to make a contribution to correcting the problems.

Any move to change things is bound to cause further disruption with increased oppressive measures from the status quo and increased rage from those who cry out for change. Yet the plain fact of the matter is that nearly every society in the world has already been altered by the technological revolution. Not only do the rich and powerful get more rich and powerful, and the poor and oppressed get more poor and oppressed, but also the fundamental social institutions of society are altered so that many customs and traditions are unable to hold the pieces together.

As a result of the technological revolution many family patterns are no longer helpful to husband, wife, and children. The basic function that women performed in traditional societies was the bearing and raising of children who could ensure the continued existence of the tribe, nation, or race. Now the continued existence of the human race depends on women and men refusing to have children in order to slow down the population explosion. The modern development of small and mobile nuclear families was necessary to industrial production, and now, in postindustrial societies, people discover that such work and life patterns are not able to bear the strains of isolation and alienation.

Some women and men are willing to face up to this and try to do something about it, beginning with their own patterns of family life. This causes tension, but it is certainly not the root cause of disruption. New life-styles of partnership are badly needed in society, for the old patterns of domination are not working even as well as they might have in a time when domination and submission was an accepted way of life between men and women, race and race, class and class, nation and nation.

Liberation is a long journey. It is a never-ending struggle by people to find out who they are and what they must become. For women and Third World people it is a journey that may have to go on for generations. But *liberation is not a passing fad.* The horizon of freedom will continue to beckon long after the current interest in the liberation movements of the twentieth century and the writing of liberation theology fades into history. As long as people are oppressed there will be a groaning for freedom, whether in actions of rebellion or in actions to build a new future of justice for all.

It is the calling of men and women to stay on that road toward freedom and to keep the freedom rumor going; to live now *as if* the world is already on its way. God intends it to be so, and it is possible to begin acting out that intention here and now. This is not always a comforting journey, but the disturbance of the Spirit is already present and it cannot be ignored. At the Grailville Conference of Women Exploring Theology in 1972 a banner was displayed on which a beautiful butterfly was portrayed, stretching its wings in preparation for flight.[37] Around it lay the remnants of its old cocoon. And splashed across the banner were the words, "You can fly, but that cocoon has got to go!"

Anticipating God's Future. For women in the church, freedom began long ago and it is time to act now, as if they are free! They are called to live now within the horizon of the New Age. The expression Paul uses to introduce this life of "provisional freedom" is *hōs mē* ("as if not"). They are to live *as if not;* as if the facts of the situation are only provisional because of the horizon of freedom. The prolepsis or anticipation of the new world is breaking in and all other aspects of life cannot be taken with utter seriousness. The gift of God's liberation in Jesus Christ is the only really serious matter.

I mean, brothers and sisters, that the appointed time has grown very short; from now on let those who have wives live as if they had none, and those who mourn as if they were not mourning, and those who are rejoicing as if they were not rejoicing. . . . (I Cor. 7:29–30.)

Paul was a man with a commission. His mission was God's Mission: To carry the gospel to the ends of the earth. Therefore, his advice always reflected a concern for spreading the gospel. If a particular action of men or women was discrediting the gospel in the eyes of a community, his first concern was to change the practice so that the real offense of the gospel could be heard. Everything else was *hōs mē;* not of ultimate seriousness. What was serious was the horizon of freedom which was breaking in; the New Age which was about to fulfill the first signs that "the universe will be set free."

It is this proleptic emphasis of Paul on the anticipation of God's future which gives a clue to the *already . . . but not yet* nature of the struggle for freedom. The Greek word *prolēpsis* means "anticipation."[38] Proleptic actions can anticipate the situation for which they work by living *as if* the situation, at least in part, has already arrived. The first dictionary definition of prolepsis is that of a chronological mistake; a dating of an event before it actually happened. It is the opposite of *anachronism,* which is a chronological mistake that dates an event after it actually happened. For a long time the church has often appeared anachronistic. Today the church is called to be a chronological mistake, but not a backward mistake. And Christians are called to make *proleptic mistakes* which establish signs of hope, horizons of the future, in the midst of the present.

There is no one way to create such signs, but it depends on where one lives, who one is, the need at hand, and the strategies available. Living *hōs mē* is more of an attitude toward life itself than a particular set of actions. It is a calling to look critically at what is going on in the world, to see the problems and then to act in such a way that the problem itself is in some way contradicted and people begin to be transformed. Many protests and demonstrations are of this nature. They press for concrete political changes, but at the same time they say that the problem has already begun to change because *"we* are changing." The act of breaking bread together as a community which crosses racial, sexual, class, and national lines is also a *proleptic* action. It not only says, "The barriers are already broken" but it also shows "forth the Lord's death until he comes" (I Cor. 11:26).

A woman who is an ordained minister also becomes a sign

of the longed-for future of liberation and equality. At the same time her action is a reminder that much of the male clerical mystique is only a provisional arrangement to be taken *hōs mē*. Her presence in the pulpit or at the Holy Table helps to symbolize the presence of a coming God who is beyond all distinctions of male and female. The singing of a hymn in which a mixture of female and male pronouns are used to speak of God and the human beings present may have the same proleptic effect. The changing of language has the power to change the way people think about and name the world, as well as being a way of demonstrating in fact that "you are all one in Christ Jesus" (Gal. 3:28).

People can become signs in small or large ways by contradicting injustice, promoting peace, and standing in solidarity with the poor. By living out new life-styles of partnership among women and men in home, society, and church they can become proleptic signs. By working in critical and concrete ways along with those who are oppressed in other nations as well as their own, they can begin to build world solidarity now. They are already free. In the light of the gospel all other arrangements are provisional. Therefore they can act freely and responsibly together for others now. This is the *horizon of freedom*—hope in the future of God which is already now breaking into our midst. Our mandate is to live out that hope so that our actions become a prolepsis of freedom so "that the closed present is broken open in a new way."[39]

In speaking about women and freedom I have been trying to describe what it might mean to *journey on the road toward freedom* with others, for others toward God's future. The clues I have given are few, because ultimately each person and community must live out their own story of the search for human liberation. Perhaps the clues I have suggested will be helpful to women and also to men in what finally becomes a journey in partnership toward human liberation. The universal *groaning for freedom* points toward suffering and service as *diakonia* with others. The *discovery of freedom* can mean a continuing and *diacritical* search for how to be human beings; real live children of God. The *horizon of freedom* leads to hope against hope in God's promise for those who seek to add their own limited efforts to the business of prolepsis; anticipating the future in the present so that they can begin to know how it feels to be free.

"I Wish I Knew How It Would Feel to Be Free," by Billy Taylor, was first sung as a hymn by members of the East Harlem Protestant Parish in New York City where I was working as a pastor. In using it in their service of worship, however, they added a last stanza:

> I'm glad I know how it does feel to be free
> I'm glad I can break all these chains holding me
> I'm glad I can say all the things I should say,
> Say 'em loud, say 'em clear, for the whole world to hear!

Why did they do this? Was the tension between the *already . . . but not yet* overcome? Of course not. In that poverty area, racism, prejudice, neglect took their daily toll of broken lives. Residents continued to be dehumanized by the welfare program of assistance. Bad schools, corrupt landlords, police brutality, narcotics addiction, and inadequate health care were grim and present facts. Yet the people of that congregation wanted to express a different reality. They wanted to sing about God's Spirit pulling them and their neighbors into a new future. Together they had found the strength to hope, and the determination to shape their future. They were free because they were beginning to create "zones of liberation" right there in East Harlem as they joined one another to realize God's future for humanity, a future where men and women can be free at last.

Together we are already on that same road toward freedom; caught in the process of liberation with only an enticing *apéritif* of the Spirit. There are many different routes toward freedom and I cannot give you, or even myself, a map. All I can do is point to Paul's haunting description of a solidarity of groaning for freedom among all our brothers and sisters of the world, and invite you who decide to be free to join in this universal symphony of groaning. In this way we can all *play our part!*

2: HUMAN LIBERATION AND THEOLOGY

Like Third World liberation theology, feminist theology is written out of an experience ⸴f oppression. It is an attempt to interpret the search for salvation as a journey toward freedom. There are as many liberation theologies as there are people committed to search for the meaning of human liberation in today's world. Wherever the rising consciousness of groups and individuals leads them to critical awareness of the contradictions in society and to actions toward change, the need arises to interpret their new understanding and actions. This challenge emerges out of particular circumstances and reflects a variety of traditions.

Yet, at the same time, for Christians there is a common motif in liberation theology. The action-reflection *(praxis)* arises out of a commitment to Jesus Christ and a desire to understand the meaning of the good news in the light of the changing world. The praxis of liberation is carried forward in a continuing dialectic of divine-human action. God's actions on behalf of humankind are the basis of reflection and insight in relation to the actions of communities on behalf of others.

There is always a tension between Christian tradition and the new experience gained by advocates of liberation in a specific situation of oppression. This tension can be the creative force of theology in which actions and experience are constantly viewed in the wider horizon of God's concern for all humankind. Interpretations of the gospel are tested by the experience of Christian communities working with others in society. The actions of the communities are also tested by the Biblical witness to the meaning and purpose of human liberation as part of God's plan for all of the groaning creation.

There is also another tension which comes from the fact that human liberation takes on meaning in particular contexts. Liberation is always experienced concretely, as individuals and groups discover ways in which they have found new "room to breathe" in society. Therefore, the various visions of the meaning of humanization and liberation reflect their own situation. Sometimes that situation clearly places one type of liberation theology at odds with another. For instance, black theology may focus on the black experience of oppression to the exclusion of the oppression of women. Feminist theology may have a focus that is quite the reverse. This tension, however, can also be creative, because it leads each group to clarify its position, and provides a variety of perspectives that can illuminate our understanding of human liberation.

The purpose of this chapter is not to assert that all people writing liberation theology say the same thing, but that the dialogue between those concerned with the praxis of freedom is an important task. In spite of much disagreement, many of the goals are held in common and need to be worked on in mutual respect and solidarity. In addition, whatever these theologies may have to say, they make a contribution to the total theological enterprise of using our minds to reflect on the meaning of God's actions in the world. While recognizing that at every point differences can be identified, it is still a significant task to reflect on *common methodology, common perspectives,* and *common themes* which are shared by many liberation theologies. These motifs can then be explored from the feminist perspective, as we join together in the exciting and challenging search for more truly human community in a Christian context.

COMMON METHODOLOGY

Liberation theologies share certain methodological ingredients of task, approach, and purpose that are important to women and men in their theological reflection. Of course, there is *no one style* of theology. Each person is free to choose the particular style that develops out of tradition, education, and life experience. The styles vary according to the premises, perspectives on reality, and types of philosophy. In spite of these differences there is a growing consensus among liberation theologians in describing their task. What they are about is doing *theo-logy:* Using their *logos* (their mind) in the perspective of God, as God is known in and through the Word in the world. Thus Gustavo Gutiérrez tells us that "theology is critical reflection—in the light of the Word accepted in faith—on historical praxis and therefore on the presence of Christians in the world."[1]

Genitive Theologies. This task is sometimes rather difficult to establish in liberation theologies because they have a tendency to be what are sometimes called genitive theologies: theologies *of* women, *of* blacks, *of* Latin Americans, etc.[2] When we speak of feminist theology, we sometimes think that it is not only *by* women but also *about* women.

Strictly speaking, feminist theology could be written *by* men. There are many men who are also actively engaged in trying to counter the prevailing oppressive situation in which both men and women are trapped. They too are advocating the equality and partnership of both sexes, and searching for new life-styles and structures in church and society.[3] However, it takes a brave man to advocate such theology in the face of the social scorn of those who would label him as "feminine," and the ideological scorn of those who declare that liberation theology, at least initially, must be written from the point of view of those who have experienced a concrete situation of social oppression.

Again, strictly speaking, feminist theology is *not* about women. It is about God. It is not a form of *"ego-logy"* in which women just think about themselves. When women do it, they speak of feminist theology in order to express the fact that the experience from which they speak and the world out of which they perceive God's words and actions and join in those actions is that of women seeking human equality. Another way of expressing this is to say that the *ecology of their theology* is that of a woman living in a particular time and place.[4]

The importance of women doing theology is the same as that of any other group around the world. They make a contribution to the *unfinished dimension* of theology. Women want to add to the understanding of the Christian faith, not to replace the other insights that have been contributed in the past. This is very important to a Christian church that has been dominated for so long by white, Western, male perspectives on God. Women add their small piece of experience about the way God is known to them to all the other pieces, so that theology becomes more wholistic and comprehensive.

Inductive Approach. In general, women, along with other liberation theologians, stress an inductive rather than a deductive approach. In the past much theology was done by deducing conclusions from first principles established out of Christian tradition and philosophy. Today many people find it more helpful to do theology by an inductive method— drawing out the material for reflection from their life experience as it relates to the gospel message. Here stress is placed on the *situation-variable* nature of the gospel. The gospel is good news to people only when it speaks concretely to their particular needs of liberation. For instance, it is no help to tell the blind woman that she can walk. Good news for the blind must deal with changing the oppressed situation of blindness.

For this reason liberation theologies recognize that persons and societies find themselves in different situations of oppression, and they try to address themselves to concrete experiences that can illuminate their own experience and can be shared with others. They try to express the gospel in the light of the experience of oppression out of which they are written, whether that be racial or sexual, social or economic, psychological or physical. Such a method draws upon the contributions of the many disciplines that help to illuminate the human condition and not just on a particular theological tradition. This point of view is reflected in Rosemary Ruether's *Liberation Theology* when she writes:

... a fuller integration of the sciences necessary for the fullest reflection on the question of human liberation today cannot be done by a single scholar. It waits upon a multi-disciplinary teamwork that can integrate the many sources of data and types of reflection and symbolization around the core of theological reflection. Only with such a multi-disciplinary integration of human sciences can we begin to speak of the basis of a theology of liberation adequate to the present human situation.[5]

This inductive approach is *experimental in nature.* It is a process of seeking out the right questions to ask and trying out different hypotheses that arise. It becomes a theology of constantly revised questions and tentative observations about a changing world, rather than the type of theology described by Thomas Aquinas as a "science of conclusions."[6] In trying to develop new models for thinking about God in a Christian context, women discover a vast quantity of questions addressed to Biblical and church tradition and to the concepts of creation, redemption, sin, salvation, and incarnation. The experimental nature of this inductive theology leaves no doctrine unchallenged in the search for a faith that can shape life amid rapid, and sometimes chaotic, change. "These doctrines are no longer taken so much as answers than as ways of formulating the questions."[7]

Such an experimental or inductive approach is very much dependent on the *corporate support* of the community of faith and action out of which it grows. Just as Latin-American liberation theology grows out of the small struggling communities working with others to face up to their revolutionary situation, so black theology grows out of the American black community and black churches. As Rubem Alves, a Brazilian theologian, says, "The seed of the future . . . [is the] community of hope."[8] This approach is also important for the corporate style of the women's movement. Not only is much of the work of women done on a multidisciplinary basis, but also in small communities who experiment together in actions and reflection both in groups and through the constant exchange of materials and ideas.

Theology as Praxis. This communal search is doubly important because liberation theology is intended to be put into practice by those who join in the search. The purpose of this type of theology is *praxis*, action that is concurrent with reflection or analysis and leads to new questions, actions, and reflections.[9] In this format theology flows out of and into action. It is a tool for doing something that can become a catalyst for change among those who believe in the Biblical promises for the oppressed. The direction of thought flows, not only "downward" from the "theological experts" but also upward and outward out of the collective experience of action and ministry.

For this reason liberation theology is not usually *systematic theology*. The purpose of doing it is not to place all the discoveries or conclusions into one overarching system, but rather to apply the discoveries to a new way of action to bring about change in society. Therefore, when things become difficult in a particular situation, or when there seems to be little immediate hope for change, people have a tendency to say: "Liberation theology is finished. It didn't work." Yet as

long as the Bible speaks of God as the Liberator of the oppressed, and as long as the situations of oppression continue
to exist, there will be those who seek ways to express their
faith and confidence in God through whatever means are
open to them.[10]

This form of *practical theology* brings action and reflection
together. As Bonhoeffer is reported to have said, "We shall
not know what we will not do." Certainly the thinking must
be systematic in that it tries to be logical, consistent, and
documented, but the purpose of the thinking and its verifica-
tion is found in praxis (action and reflection), and not in the
writing of fat volumes of systematic theology. Ethics and
application are not simply the ways of relating thought to
social situations, because the thought itself is denied if it does
not arise in the context of action. Gutiérrez underlines this
point in saying, "All the political theologies, the theologies of
hope, of revolution, and of liberation, are not worth one act
of genuine solidarity with exploited classes."[11]

Whatever the movement, be it a Third World or Fourth
World, if its focus is on human liberation, its inductive methodology will be one of thinking about God in the light of
concrete oppressive experiences in order to find ways to
express the purpose and plan of God for creation in the
building of a more humane society.

COMMON PERSPECTIVES

In addition to a common inductive and experimental
methodology, liberation theologies also share at least three
common perspectives in reflection on the experience of God
in the world.

Biblical Promise. The first perspective is that the Biblical
promises of liberation are an important part of theological
reflection. Two major motifs of the Bible are those of *liberation* and *universality*.[12] God is portrayed in both the Old and

New Testaments as the Liberator, the one who sets people free. God is not just the liberator of one small nation or group, but of all of humankind. This theme of liberation is, of course, not the only theme, but it is an important part of the Biblical understanding of God's *oikonomia* or action for the world in the history of salvation. Joseph Comblin writes:

The theologians of liberation theology do not say that the Bible teaches a doctrine of liberation for all men [and women] of every age, of all time, and all nations. But they are convinced that in the world we have today the Bible's precept of charity can be interpreted only through a theology of liberation. Any other interpretation would fall short of the demands of charity as it is presented in the Bible. Those theologians aren't in the slightest claiming that their reading of the Bible is valid for all times. But they say it is the right one for the society we live in today—and that is all that matters.[13]

God's *oikonomia* or plan for the world provides an eschatological perspective concerning the future of humanity. Because Christians see themselves as part of "God's utopia" they participate in the work of liberation. Paul points out in I Cor. 9:17 that they are "entrusted with a commission *(oikonomia).*" Participation in God's work is the way in which they express hope and confidence in God's intention of liberation and salvation for the whole inhabited world *(oikoumenē).* No longer are lines drawn between Christian and non-Christian, or between one confession and another. Instead, Christians join with all those involved in the revolution of freedom, justice, and peace. As Moltmann writes, "It is time now for all the different freedom movements to cooperate in a brotherly [and sisterly] way, for the misery of humankind has not become less urgent."[14]

Liberation theology places stress on the fact that the Gospels tell of the good news of liberation. Christ has set the captives free and, therefore, there is future and hope. This hope stems, not just from human actions and strategies that are often weak and misguided, but from God's promise for all humanity. Ernst Käsemann says:

I see the whole of the New Testament as involving the cause of Christian freedom, and I have done my best to show that the cause is developed in much diversity, because it exists only in terms of practical mundane affairs, in relation to Christian selflessness, stupidity, misrepresentation and denial, and changes its spearhead from time to time.[15]

In the women's liberation movement there has been a lot of rejection of the Bible as the basis for theology because of the patriarchal, cultural attitudes that it reveals.[16] Yet those who would do Christian theology cannot abandon the story of Jesus of Nazareth. They find instead that they must use the best tools of scholarship to wrestle with the texts, and to find how liberation and universality apply to their own experience of longing and groaning for freedom.[17]

World as History. The second perspective is that of the world as history. Most liberation theologies are written from the modern point of view that both humanity and the world are to be understood as historical, as both changing and changeable.[18] The Bible views the world as a series of meaningful events that are moving toward the fulfillment of God's plan and purpose of salvation.[19] In the same way, modern thinkers view the world as events that are subject to human intervention, planning, and change. Each human being is made up of her or his individual history, and society is formed out of collective events or histories.

To view the world as history is to think of it not just as a record of past events but also as a process of change from past, to present, to future. This is a process that takes on meaning through the interpretation of events that shape our future.[20] The future that evolves out of the past *(futurum)* is placed at the disposal of women and men who are aware of their own historical possibility and seek out political, economic, and social ways or planning for tomorrow. For Christians there is also a vision of a future that comes toward us *(adventus)* and that God places at our disposal.[21] Through *hoping* in the coming of God's future they find new courage and strength to enter into the difficult process of *planning* and acting on behalf of human liberation.

For Christian women the planning of the future as *futurum* must be based on the "rewriting of history" to include "herstory" in the total picture of the way history has evolved. Out of the strength gained from past accomplishments and the warnings of past defeats comes a new energy to be put to use in changing the social realities of oppression that they face. At the same time, "the horizon of hope" in God's coming future *(adventus)* prevents discouragement and disillusionment when the struggle for liberation is frustrated by powerful, androcentric social attitudes. They enter into the struggle without any guarantee of success, knowing that not only their sisters and brothers but they themselves will often stand in the way of the development of a humane society of partnership. Women enter the struggle because they hope in God's promise of liberation and because according to Dorothee Sölle they are driven by the knowledge that the "Gospel's business is the liberation of human beings. . . . Having faith, we put our wager on the liberation of all people."[22] They continue the struggle because to be human is to take part in this historical process or *historicity* and to have an opportunity of transforming the world and shaping the future.[23]

To view the world as history is to become involved in the development of ideologies or sets of ideas that can be used to change and shape this reality. Christians, along with others, make use of these interpretations of reality and history in order to participate in "the revolutions of freedom." Christian women make use of the ideology of women's liberation. Black liberation theology owes much of its perspective on reality to the ideology of the black liberation movement.

Many Latin Americans look to some socialist ideology to provide helpful conceptual tools for change.[24]

The difficulty of this dangerous but important "mix" between faith and ideology is that all ideologies are only partial and, therefore, distorted descriptions of social reality. Yet ideologies gain their power to change the actions and thoughts of human beings just because of their intention to change the situation in line with that one set of ideas.[25] For Christians all ideologies must be subject to constant critique in the light of the gospel. In fact, they do not know exactly what the future will be like. Neither God nor ideologies provide them with a "blueprint." God's promise leads to a confidence that the future is open, but not to an exact knowledge of how liberation will be accomplished or what it will look like.

Because ideologies are helpful in dealing with and shaping the *futurum,* they play an important part in liberation movements. Yet they are always partial in the light of faith in God's coming *adventus* and they present a danger for those who must live with "humble agnosticism" about the future. Women, like other people, are often swept up in the currents of ideology, yet as Christians they remain an undependable part of liberation movements, because they must live by the horizon of the *adventus* and not by a blind commitment to any ideology.[26]

Liberation theologies view the world as history and make use of ideologies because their purpose is to participate with God in changing the world to advocate the right of oppressed people to share in building their own "house of freedom." The impact of this common perspective can be seen clearly in the actions of Christian women both in the church and in society. For instance, the Women's Caucus at the General Assembly of the National Council of Churches which was held at Detroit in 1969 presented a statement to the Assembly which reflects this point of view.

Women's oppression and women's liberation is a basic part of the struggle of blacks, browns, youth, and others. We will not be able to create a new church and a new society until and unless women are full participants. We intend to be full participants. . . .

So women are rising; that is our first point. We are rising, black and white, red and brown, to demand change, to demand humanity for ourselves as well as others. . . .

Secondly, we wish to present some facts which illustrate the situation of women. Nowhere is the situation of women better illustrated than in our male-dominated and male-oriented churches.[27]

Salvation as a Social Event. The third shared perspective of liberation theologies is that of salvation as a social event. In Christian theology today there is a new awareness of human beings in their body, mind, and spirit and in their social relationships with others.[28] This has led to a broadening of the understanding of individual salvation in the afterlife to include the beginnings of salvation in the lives of men and women in society. Often the Old Testament concept of salvation as *shalom* or wholeness and total social well-being in community with others is stressed.[29]

Emphasis is placed upon the longed-for eternal life as a quality of existence in the *here and now*. It is expressed through the actions of sharing God's gift of liberation and blessing with all people. In a historical view of the world, salvation is not an escape from fated nature, but rather the power and possibility of transforming the world, restoring creation, and seeking to overcome suffering. This stress is especially clear among those searching for ways of expressing the gospel message as good news for the oppressed, the hungry, the alienated of our own sorry world. In liberation theology salvation is understood as good news because it includes concrete social liberation in oppressive situations. James Cone states:

Because God's act for . . . [humanity] involves . . . [human] liberation from bondage, . . . [human] response to God's grace of liberation is an act for . . . brothers and sisters who are oppressed. There can be no reconciliation with God unless the hungry are fed, the sick are healed, and justice is given to the poor.[30]

In this perspective sin also takes on a different meaning. Sin as the opposite of liberation is seen as *oppression*, a situation in which there is no community, no room to live as a whole human being. Dorothee Sölle reminds us that sin cannot be understood only as a private matter. "Sin to us is eminently a political, a social term."[31] It includes the sins of our own people, race, and class in which we participate. Therefore, we are faced with responsibility not only for admitting our collaboration in such social sin, but also for working to change the social structures that bring it about. Ruether describes this responsibility in saying:

We need to build a new cooperative social order out beyond the principles of hierarchy, rule and competitiveness. Starting in the grass-roots local units of human society where psycho-social polarization first began, we must create a living pattern of mutuality between men and women, between parents and children, among people in their social, economic and political relationships and, finally, between humankind and the organic harmonies of nature.[32]

There are probably other perspectives shared by many women and other people working out liberation theologies in an experimental way, but at least these three (Biblical promises of liberation; world as history; salvation as a social event) are important to their praxis. Feminist theology is not alone in bringing these perspectives to bear in the dialogue between faith and the world, but it has a part to play in contributing to the ongoing development of a more complete theology.

COMMON THEMES

Liberation theologies arise out of concrete circumstances in every part of the globe. These circumstances give rise to a wide variety of "accents" and themes. Yet some common themes, along with common methodology and common perspectives, can be identified that are also important in feminist theology.

Humanization. One theme of the gospel of liberation, which emerges as a matter for constant action-reflection, is that of humanization. In situations of broken community, of oppression, of defuturized minorities and majorities there is a constant longing to be a whole human being. In society people are so often treated as *things* that they become pawns of social fate, unable to exercise their human ability to shape their own world in community with others. These people express the longing and alienation both destructively and constructively as they search for ways to change their condition, or for ways to escape out of this world. In their hearts and communities they really do wish they knew "how it would feel to be free!"

There is no one definition of what it means to be human. Each culture or subculture, each ideology, each religion explains the reality of human nature in its own way. One person's freedom or dignity may not be the same as another's. In Maoist China people work to create a new social human being. Third World groups in the United States are creating a new understanding of human dignity and worth by seeking the heritage of their past. Psychologists and social scientists present varying and conflicting views of human nature. Women search for a way to combine their biological and cultural identity as women with an affirmation of full partnership in humanity. In spite of the variety of understandings, the social definition of human worth and dignity is of crucial importance for every person seeking wholeness and meaning in life.

Although there is no one definition of what it means to be human, it seems clear that some of the key factors are to be discovered in the area of human relationships of love, freedom, and respect. Human beings need *support communities* in order to find out who they are. The task of finding who they are can only be done by themselves. They are the ones who must build their own house of freedom. Yet at the same time they can only find their own sense of being and worth in community with others. Human beings need some *possibility of participation* in understanding and shaping the world in which they live. They are "historificators," those who become themselves in building their own individual and collective history and world. Human beings need to be *accepted as subjects* and not as things or objects of someone else's manipulation. They are not simply functions or roles in society and organizations.

For this reason the writers of the Vatican II "Pastoral Constitution on the Church in the Modern World" *(Gaudium et Spes)* relate their concern for equality and reverence for the human person to the search for social justice.

. . . with respect to the fundamental rights of the person, every type of discrimination, whether social or cultural, whether based on sex, race, color, social conditions, language, or religion, is to be overcome and eradicated as contrary to God's intent. For in truth it must still be regretted that fundamental personal rights are not yet being universally honored. Such is the case of a woman who is denied the right and freedom to choose a husband, to embrace a state of life, or to acquire an education or cultural benefits equal to those recognized by men.[33]

Biblical anthropology seems to indicate that a human being is to be understood as a subject of God's love and concern and, therefore, as a responsible subject of her or his own individual and collective actions. Just as God is known through actions in history, so women and men are known and understood by their activity in creating their world and their history.[34] As responsible persons they are known through what they do and how they think and act. If this is so, then there are many ways of being human, for people are human in relation to history and the world in which they live and with which they interact.

One of the struggles of women and Third World peoples is to demand freedom to be human in just this sense. They are not interested in being defined simply in terms of categories of race or sex. These categories have been used against them in a racist and sexist world that tends to perpetuate the myth that white, Western males are more fully human. One seldom hears references to a "white engineer" or a "male minister." Yet one does hear statements about a "black engineer" or a "woman minister." Whatever people do, it is not necessary to label it with biological categories if they are all equally members of the human race.

For Christians the most important image of humanity is Jesus Christ who was incarnate in human flesh so that we might know God's intention for humanity. In Christ we see a human being able to relate to people in love, regardless of how society has defined their being or status. In Christ we also see an integration of word and deed so that love, righteousness, and obedience were lived as well as spoken.[35] It is this lived relationship that helps to inspire Christian men and women to join others in integrating their words and deeds of love and liberation.

In liberation theologies we see the attempt to follow the injunction of Jesus to "continue in my word . . . and you will know the truth, and the truth will make you free" (John 8:31–32). In the integration of thought and action there is a constant attempt to find out more fully the nature of the incarnation and of true humanity. Gutiérrez writes:

It is important to keep in mind that beyond—or rather, through—the struggle against misery, injustice, and exploitation the goal is the *creation of a new man* [and woman]. . . . This aspiration to create a new . . . [human] is the deepest motivation in the struggle which many have undertaken in Latin America.[36]

Conscientization. Another important theme, which emerges out of the analysis of the world as history, is that of conscientization. If human beings have responsibility for shaping their own individual and social history, then they need a process of coming to self-awareness that helps them to learn their own potential for action in shaping the world. This process of coming to new consciousness and new ability to take action has become popularly known as *conscientization.* The word is current in Latin-American theology and has been popularized in Brazil and other countries by the writings of such people as Helder Camara, Paulo Freire, and Gustavo Gutiérrez.

According to Freire, conscientization is an *ongoing process* of "learning to perceive social, economic and political contradictions and to take action against the oppressive elements of reality."[37] It is not an educational methodology or technique, for the way to go about doing this might be quite different among Brazilian peasants, Hong Kong city dwellers, or middle-class women. Rather it is a description of the importance of coming to awareness about the particular world in which people dwell in order to contradict the dehumanizing elements in that world. Nor is conscientization just a psychological technique for helping people "feel better." Its built-in purpose is collective social involvement, leading to personal and social change.

With the worldwide expansion of technology, communications, and transportation there is a "revolution of rising consciousness," not only among the "consciousness-raising" groups of women, but also in every corner of the globe.

Everywhere people look to their religious or cultural heritage to help them express the convictions that *they are somebody* and that they have a share in the world. This process can easily lead to disillusionment and bitterness or become frozen into another type of bureaucratic reform. Yet at the same time, when it is a continuing process of new actions (however small) and new reflections and learning, it expresses a way in which people can participate in developing their own future as *futurum*. By reflecting on and working in this process of conscientization, liberation theologies can aid oppressed peoples to join in the affirmative chant used in black liberation rallys in the United States: "I am Somebody. . . . I am Somebody. . . . I am Somebody!"

Dialogue and Community. The third theme, which emerges out of search for social salvation and liberation, is that of dialogue and community-building. Liberation theologies do not spend all their time talking about the oppressors and oppressed as though liberation is a simple process of identifying a common enemy and reversing the roles. Ruether emphasizes this in saying: "What this means is that one cannot dehumanize the oppressors without ultimately dehumanizing oneself, and aborting the possibilities of the liberation movement into an exchange of roles of oppressor and oppressed."[38]

Liberation theologies of all types are aware that sin, produced by social contradictions in church and society, results in new barriers of mistrust and polarization between individuals and groups. In response to this, many people are searching for new ways of dialogue among groups of Christians and non-Christians, as well as groups in the First, Second, Third, and Fourth Worlds.[39] Such dialogue can be based only on mutual trust and the devising of shared tasks and not just on "monologues" about doctrines, ideologies, and dominance. This type of dialogue is well described by Paulo Freire as an encounter between people, mediated by the world in order to name and transform the world.[40]

Dialogue or the building of new human community calls for overcoming *vertical violence* between oppressors and oppressed: men and women; rich and poor; white and black; ministers and laity. The structures that cause sexism, classism, racism, and clericalism are violent by their very nature, and they evoke counterviolence unless there is a new way to work together for change.

Oppressed groups are not in a position to dialogue with the oppressor groups because the process of dialogue only functions where there is a situation of equality and trust. "If you want to talk with me, take your foot off of my neck!" First, the oppressed groups must develop their own power base of mutual support, new identity, and new possibility for collective action. They must search together for their own liberation according to their own agenda, because liberation is not a commodity to be given away. It is a process of new awareness and action that grows out of new personal and collective consciousness.

For this reason, dialogue depends on the overcoming of the *horizontal violence* used by oppressed groups to express their own frustrations and their low opinion of themselves and of one another by putting each other down and selling out to the image of their inferiority projected on them by the existing status quo of society.[41] This often happens in developing countries where "new elites" emulate the colonialists in despising and oppressing their own people. It happens among American blacks who turn their rage on one another in competing for the crumbs left over from white consumption or in turning their internal rage into destruction of their own ghetto community. It happens among women who defeat one another and mistrust each other rather than learning to be *pro-woman* so that they can become *pro-human*. In the case of women's liberation it is well known that women are often their own worst enemies as outspoken supporters of the status quo. Mary Daly writes: "The new consciousness implied in sisterhood requires an ejection by women of the images internalized in patriarchal society which limit their aspirations and turn them against themselves and each other."[42]

As oppressed groups begin to develop their own identity and power in overcoming horizontal violence they know that eventually the structures of society and church that result in vertical violence have to be changed. Only in this way can a new form of human life be born in which both the oppressor and the oppressed are liberated from the former structures that have polarized and dehumanized both groups. Liberation theology seeks to deal not only with the fact of social, political, and economic barriers but also with the reality of the ultimate intention of God that all people be reconciled with one another.[43]

Women and men, black and white, poor and rich have to move into a new relationship with each other in which oppressor groups are not only advocates of the oppressed but also willing to come to a new understanding of how their access to power perpetuates the old social contradictions. Out of the self-liberation of oppressed groups can grow a possibility of shared world and tasks and new forms of dialogue. Dialogue becomes possible when members of both groups begin to see a new shared task in which they have some form of equality in working together. Around a specific action in changing a particular social structure or custom it is possible to dialogue—but only if the oppressor groups see that the way to accomplish change is to respond to the leadership and initiative of the oppressed and to work together in transforming the world.

A new position of consciousness, confidence, and leadership can give women and Third World people an opportunity to dialogue in a relationship of equality and growing trust. Such a situation is particularly important for women and men because women live daily with their oppressors. Women live with men, work with men and are men's mothers. They have to take initiative in new forms of partnership and dialogue if they are going to help men change the social structures and customs that are often so dehumanizing.

Contrary to popular myth, women who advocate women's liberation are frequently happily married mothers who, nevertheless, are aware of the deep pain which comes into the relationships of family and work when there is no communication or partnership. Together with each other and also with their husbands, friends, and employers, their goal is first to become feminists themselves, second to help men become feminists; and last to carry on genuine dialogue so that the world will be transformed to the point where no feminists (male or female) are needed because there *is* social, economic, and political equality of the sexes who become equally human.

Liberation theologies, including feminist theologies, are particularly important to the life and health of the church. Here, sexism, racism, and classism have been legitimatized by hierarchical ecclesiastical structures as well as by doctrinal teachings. In such a situation there is little hope for dialogue, let alone for community, until the structures of oppression are confronted and transformed into a situation of true partnership. The church seems to be one of the last institutions in society to hear and respond to its own Gospel mandate for living in a New Age "to preach good news to the poor . . . proclaim release to the captives . . . to set at liberty those who are oppressed" (Luke 4:18).

Women form the vast majority of those who find themselves oppressed in Christian communities. Yet hope for change and renewal of the church for the world can come only as new forms of human community, new life-styles are developed which eliminate domination and submission and express cooperation. As this begins to happen, women will be set free to use their God-given gifts in the service of ministry for others.

In the Christian perspective, liberation theologies lift up

common methodologies, perspectives, and themes that can help women and men on all six continents to develop a more complete theology. Certainly these approaches are not the only ones, yet they can make a contribution to the doing of theology as a way of acting and reflecting on what it means to be a Christian and a human being in concrete social situations.

Their themes arise, along with others, out of a deep human longing to be free from oppression. They are not new, for they find many echoes in the Biblical story of a creation and a people groaning for liberation. In another age we might have talked more about salvation instead of the process of *conscientization* and conversion; of incarnation instead of the search for *humanization;* or of communion instead of *dialogue and community.* Now we must talk of our common faith and our common world in whatever way that illuminates our common task together as women and men in a Christian context.

3: SEARCH
FOR A USABLE PAST

Human beings need to find identity and strength from the images of past history which can help to guide them in shaping their present and future. Such a past that is still living, evolving, and meaningful is not always easy to find. Some persons and groups are ignorant or ashamed of their past. Others have a history that is full of sorrow and pain. But, whatever the past may be, it becomes a *usable past* through reflection on its meaning and mistakes in such a way that human beings build a common sense of direction toward the future. Research into the hidden past of oppressed people frees them to gain a sense of history on which to build their future. Combined with a contemporary history of actions to change their world, such a usable past helps in the search for a *usable future.*[1]

Liberation theology can help in the search for a usable past because it seeks to reflect on the love of God in Jesus Christ as the basis of the future. It can aid us in seeking out the *Tradition* of Jesus Christ in our lives, not only from the past events of his life, death, and resurrection, but also from the present and future events of his liberating power. Because we remember the past and live with it as the promise of the future, we have a *memory of the future* which God is bringing toward us. It is this memory of the future which makes us "prisoners of hope" (Zech. 9:12).

Our hope is focused on the future, but draws strength and

meaning from the events of the past and present. These events form the *tradition* which guides our actions and gives meaning to our existence. Yet tradition in human life and in Christian life is a "two-edged sword." It can provide a usable past with which to join in shaping a usable future and be a firm "stepping-stone" toward human liberation. At the same time it can also become a useless past which provides a false identity or "millstone" which prevents us from joining the struggle toward that future for which all humanity is longing. With such a useless past the future often is seen as useless.

One of the problems of human liberation that is faced by all liberation theologies is how to deal creatively and faithfully with tradition. How do we seek out the usable past which strengthens participation in shaping a usable future? Often the work of action-reflection does not deal sufficiently with the importance of reflecting, not only on the action itself, but also on the tradition which provides perspective on God's future. Thus, if we are to continue to pursue the methodology associated with liberation theology, it is necessary to examine the problem of tradition in relation to a *usable future* and a *usable history,* as well as a *usable language* which can help to communicate Tradition in present contexts of oppression and groaning.

USABLE FUTURE

In the later part of the twentieth century the question of reality and meaning in the light of the future brings to the fore the questionableness of tradition. The patterns of cultural heritage which make up the historical nature of human beings are crumbling in the face of unprecedented rapidity of change. Furthermore, those who search for reality and authenticity more often than not turn toward the present and future, casting off what they consider to be shackles of the past. Not only the traditions of men, but also the whole Christian Tradition is called radically into question. Is it authentic? Does it have any meaning for us today? Does it bind our future by its existence?

Such questioning is not new, for theology has been struggling with the question of reality since ancient times. In modern history Immanuel Kant's famous questions about what man and woman can know, what they ought to do, and for what they may hope have shaped theological and philosophical concerns.[2] More and more the third question of hope has become the key question of reality in a world moving so fast toward possible destruction. This shift in point of view has affected the way modern theologians are seeking to deal with the problem of tradition.

Structural Element of Human Existence. Recent currents in the ecumenical discussion of tradition are marked by the discovery that *tradition is a problem* in the light of historicity. Since World War II there has been increased discussion of tradition in the social field where scholars have tried to understand the relation of the "revolutionary world" to prewar history. In Protestant circles there has been a rediscovery of tradition as an important element in theology, and in Roman Catholic circles theologians have begun to realize that an explicit theology of tradition is a recent nineteenth-century development.

Both Protestant and Roman Catholic scholars have been attempting to find a common understanding of tradition as expressed in both written and unwritten forms. Recognizing that both Scripture and tradition are forms of the traditioning of the gospel of Jesus Christ, they have begun to emphasize distinctions *within* the meaning of the word "tradition." In historical and theological investigations, distinctions are being made between *Tradition* (the handing over of Jesus Christ, Matt. 17:22; Rom. 8:31–32), and *traditions* (particular confessional patterns).

The Faith and Order study of the World Council of Churches on *Tradition and Traditions,* completed in 1963, summarizes an ecumenical consensus that distinguishes between tradition, traditions, and *the* Tradition (or, Tradition).[3] In this report, "tradition" refers to the total traditioning process that operates in human history and society; "traditions" refer to the patterns of church life, such as confessions, liturgies, polities, etc., that have developed in each confessional church group; *the* Tradition refers to Christ as the content of the traditioning process by which God hands Christ over to men and women.[4]

These definitions tend to shift and change according to the context of the usage and to the intent of a particular writer. In spite of the variations there is fairly wide ecumenical support for this general type of distinction and it is helpful to make use of it as a methodological tool for examining the search for a usable past. On the Roman Catholic side, Yves Congar gives his own specific definitions of the typology, but he does make use of such distinctions and even dedicates the second half of his book *Tradition and Traditions* to the Faith and Order study and to those who worked on the same problem at the Second Vatican Council.[5]

The importance of tradition is being recognized and investigated as a *basic anthropological category* related to historicity or change as the medium of human existence. In the writings of such theologians as Gerhard Ebeling the shift from the primary system of static ontological categories of thought to the secondary system of changing, historical categories of thought and action is clearly reflected.[6] This approach turns from the primary system view of the Middle Ages which understands tradition as a deposit of the ancient past, to the secondary system view of the modern world which understands tradition as meaningful events that call for commitment in shaping the present and the future.

Tradition as a basic anthropological category is thus understood as *the structural element of human existence in which the still living and evolving past calls for commitment in shaping human community in the present and future.*

The apperception of tradition as a component of human existence which constantly makes use of past experience and events in order to shape the present and future is an important tool for liberation theology. It gives those who are oppressed or seeking to change the status quo a means for sifting out history in order to reject those elements which form the ideologies and myths of oppression against which they struggle. In this understanding of tradition can be discovered the means for rejecting the useless past in favor of a usable past. Such a process is constantly going forward as both a conscious and unconscious part of human nature. In liberation theology, which views the world and humanity as historical and changing, traditioning can be seen as a process of conscientization or coming to awareness of one's self and world in order to transform it together with others. This process can be used *intentionally* in order to provide a means of participation in shaping a more humane tradition that points toward a usable future for all humanity.

Tradition as Mission. When we take a new look at tradition in the light of the shifting emphases outlined above we see that Tradition (in its particular sense of handing over Jesus Christ) and God's Mission belong to the same theological spectrum. Both of them are dependent on the action of God in Christ; both have living, active, sending quality which calls for decision concerning present and future; both find their clarification, not in polemics, but in differentiation between root understanding in God's action, and the derivative understandings in the various activities of men and women. The nature of mission as *missio Dei* (the Mission of God) is understood in Biblical perspective as the sending action and *oikonomia* (plan of salvation) of God in the history of the world. The church participates in this Mission by its missionary or sending activity in the world. Tradition is another way of describing this sending activity of God in which men and women participate through the shaping of traditions and of history.[7]

According to Biblical investigations of tradition the basis of *paradosis* (tradition) in the New Testament is God's action in Jesus Christ (Rom. 8:31–32). Karl Barth has suggested that before anything happened in the life story of Jesus, God handed him over to men and women. This action of God is the "aboriginal *traditum*" which "stands at the center of the New Testament, as the chief topic of both the apostolic kerygmata and doxologies."[8] The deliverance of Jesus is part of God's eternal plan to redeem humanity. "The Son of man is to be delivered *(paradidosthai)* into the hands of men." (Matt. 17:22.) The origin of all *paradosis* is found in God's *paradosis* by which the Son becomes "the first object and bearer of all salvific tradition."[9] Christ continues the traditioning process through the witness of the apostles and the inspiration of the Holy Spirit.[10] This Spirit, which is "poured out," inaugurating the Messianic Age, inspires the Tradition in human hearts so that it continues to be living, dynamic, and missionary.

In the light of some recent currents in the discussion of Tradition and Mission it is possible to say that *Tradition is Mission* because its very description is that of God's missionary activity in handing Christ over into the hands of men and women in order that all people may come to the truth (I Tim. 2:4). *The Tradition is thus seen as God's handing over of Jesus Christ into the hands of all generations and nations until Christ hands all things back to God.* The action of traditioning is seen in God's missionary activity in sending Christ. The object of the activity is Christ himself. The means by which people participate in the traditioning is by sharing in the receiving and passing on of Christ. The location of God's concern and action in sending Christ is the world, in order to bring a "new creation." When the end and goal of the traditioning action is completed, Christ will hand himself and all things back to God (Matt. 24:14; I Cor. 15:24–28).

The understanding of Tradition as God's handing over Christ to all generations and nations is another key concept in the work of liberation theologies. It serves to underline the importance of the Biblical promises of liberation by pointing to the dynamic power of God's action in the world. God has acted and is acting on behalf of humankind to break open the established structures of the status quo. Those who are oppressed look to this continued traditioning action as the basis of their memory of hope. In the past God has broken into history to liberate people from bondage to themselves and to their historical situation. It is this Tradition as Mission, constantly breaking through oppressive human traditions, that becomes the central theme of a usable past, pointing toward hope in a future which God will make usable. This provides the possibility of joining God's traditioning process by creating usable language and actions which allow the gospel to be heard as good news for *all* generations and nations.

Tradition in Liberation Theology. The various forms of liberation theology are frequently seen as a *threat to tradition* by those who do not wish to see it broken open in new ways. Looked at from the point of view of confessional *traditions* this certainly appears to be true. For instance, Marga Bührig in writing about "Discrimination Against Women" asks of the churches, "Will they realize that their mission as regards the partnership of men and women is also a break with tradition, or will they just cling to 'sacrosanct traditions' in this respect?"[11] Liberation theology is a threat to these traditions because they need to be challenged when they perpetuate a past that is unusable to a particular group of Christians. For instance, the restrictions of a woman's role at the altar so that she is considered unable to preside at the Sacrament of the Lord's Supper is based on a useless past; namely, the prohibitions against blood which render a woman "unclean" because of her biological functions.

Looked at from the point of view of tradition as a deposit of faith *(paratheke)* which has to be guarded, liberation theology is also a threat. Yet there is ample Biblical evidence to show that it was only later in the New Testament that this static idea of tradition emerged (Jude 3; I Tim. 6:20).[12] Seen from the root meaning of *paradosis,* Tradition is not a block of content to be carefully guarded by authorized hierarchies, but a dynamic action of God's love which is to be passed on to others of all sexes and races.

Looked at as a description of God's Mission of extending Christ's love to all people, Tradition is not in the least threatened by liberation theologies. Their purpose is to make that love known as God's will to bring liberation, justice, peace, and reconciliation to all creation. Because God continues to be actively present in the world through Tradition, women and men are set free to share in that action by handing the Tradition over to others rather than guarding it for one small group. In this sense liberation theology stands as a reminder that the dynamic of God's Tradition transcends and judges all human traditions and actions. In the same way liberation theology does not stand in the way of tradition as a structural element of human existence. Its very methodology makes use of the dynamic of a still living and evolving past in order to shape a usable future.

There are dangers, however, inherent in liberation theology. It is sometimes very difficult to be *faithful to Tradition* because of many experiences of the misuse of tradition in church and society. Often the tradition that has been carried forward as the still usable past by the supporters of the status quo turns out to be a useless past to those who have been excluded from participation in shaping their own future. The misuse of tradition and traditions as a way of legitimatizing the rights and privileges of a white, Western, male majority sometimes leads to polemical distortion of tradition. Such misuse of tradition to create new forms of legitimatization and polemics should be avoided. A clear understanding of the central Tradition in Christ and of the nature of the human traditioning process can help liberation theology to discern the liberating core of the Christian faith so that it can witness to this faith in particular and concrete circumstances of oppression.

It is not necessary for Third World people and women who

are Christians to develop a new religion and create new gods in order to liberate themselves. A return to pre-Biblical nature religions or insistence on a God who is literally black or female is not a necessary part of liberation theology, although it may be helpful in a process of building up self-identity. Rather than abandoning the Biblical faith of our forefathers and foremothers, liberation theology has the opportunity to mine the riches of the faith by becoming *radical*. Radicals are those who penetrate to the root of the matter. In this case it is possible to recover the true meaning of Tradition as God's sending of Christ and look to Christ's power to be present in struggling to speak and act the good news in the present and future.

The *action-reflection* methodology of liberation theology can also be a valuable asset in searching out the usable past which can help to shape the future. Out of the reflection on Tradition, traditions, and tradition in the light of concrete situations can come new models for thought and action. Such a methodology does not lead liberation theology away from the basic *paradosis*, but helps it continue in the liberating action of God's Mission in the world. This opens the way for the discovery of the presence of the living Tradition and sets people free to take risks in shaping the future.

USABLE HISTORY

If tradition is the still living and evolving past used to shape the future, the question immediately arises, What if you do not have a past? On the one hand, it is easy to point out that *every* human being has a past as a structural element of human existence which is related to her or his present and future. Yet, on the other hand, many individuals are not sufficiently aware of their past to gain enough identity and ego strength to face the stress of life. They may not know how to care because they have not experienced deep caring and love from others. Or they may not know who they are as persons because they have lacked a community and role models with which to identify.[13] Even those who have a past that they would like to forget need to learn from it because, otherwise, the factors ignored may continue to shape their lives in hidden ways.

Oppressed groups may have been systematically taught that their history, their culture, their perceptions of the world do not count, so that they see the world only through the eyes of the dominant oppressive cultural environment.[14] This later problem is doubly difficult for women in most societies. For not only has tradition been shaped in such a way as to limit their options and access to a usable present and future, but they also have no cultural tradition of their own. Almost all existing historical records have been preserved by men who defined women's roles and functions for them. For instance, "one can hardly imagine a broad study of American religion that includes past and present women."[15] At least oppressed Third World groups can seek back to find dignity and hope in the struggles, longings, and accomplishments of their ancestors for freedom. Thus James Cone has shown the history of African slaves in America as a story of deep faith and hope against hope which preserved human dignity in the face of the inhumanity of their white owners.[16]

Awareness of their own history and struggles is frequently nonexistent among women as a group. Yet it is toward such a search for a *usable history* that they must turn to build a still living and evolving past in order to shape their future as partners in society. "We create a history in which man is no longer the measure," historian Gerda Lerner writes, "but *men* and *women* are the measure."[17] This attempt to re-create a usable past as *her-story* and not just *his-story* is part of a widespread development in the modern world. All peoples searching for new identity and liberation seek out ways to shape the future by turning to history as a medium of human liberation. It is this discovery of the *meaning in his-*

tory as a bearer of living tradition which we need to investigate before turning briefly to look at the *invisible histories* in Christian tradition, and the importance of both *myth and history* in the struggle for a usable past.

Meaning in History. In the modern world, history has taken on increased importance as a means of self-definition and description of reality. Women and men find that they are threatened, not primarily by the natural forces of the cosmos, but by their own historical power that threatens the cosmos and so "drags all reality into history."[18] Ebeling summarizes the context of all modern thinking, including the theological discussion of tradition and liberation, when he says:

For modern man everything, the whole of reality turns to history. . . .

Whatever problem that is taken up, it transforms itself, at all events in the first instance, into a historical problem.[19]

Men and women see themselves free to shape their world and, therefore, interpret the world in terms of possibility and future. The reality of the world as people experience it is thus historicized. Its very nature is not of static, natural substance, but of dynamic historical existence. Natural objects themselves find their meaning in relation to their use in the process of history. The world is viewed in terms of functional, action-oriented categories. This interpretation of *human beings and their world understood as a meaningful process is usually called historicity.*

The general use of the term "historicity" to describe a particular world view or way of experiencing reality that has become characteristic of the modern age can best be discussed in detail by looking at the three "modes of history" which it is intended to include. These three modes represent distinctions which can be made in German, but which become confused in English usage.

The first term is *Historie*. This word, translated in English by the word "history," refers to a chronicle or narrative of *facts*. It was a particularly influential way of looking at history in nineteenth-century historicism which held that historical reality included only the facts that could be proved by "scientific" methods of criticism. If the ideology of historicism is avoided, *Historie* can be employed as a critical method of studying past events and becomes valuable for examining the past. Such methods, employed by modern historical disciplines in the same way as in other fields of modern research, not only provide valuable information needed by women and men to shape their future but also serve the important function of constantly raising questions about all assumptions and ideologies so that new ways of understanding the world are always possible. By open and critical investigation of *Historie*, people are emancipated from those facts because they perceive the "myths" they contain. Moltmann thus speaks of *Historie* as an "iconoclasm of hope turned backwards."[20]

The second term included in the general category of historicity is *Geschichte*. This word is also translated in English by the word "history," but it refers to history as *events* which continue to have meaning and can be interpreted by those involved in the events. This term has taken on great importance for twentieth-century theologians as they have reacted against *historicism* by pointing out that bare facticity in history is at best provisional, and always open to new interpretation in the light of new discoveries, new methods, and new value systems.[21] Women and men are historical beings and not just facts. They are responders to and creators of facts who are constantly involved with them at the point of their meaning or eventfulness.

The third term included in the general category of historicity is *Geschichtlichkeit*. This word is translated into English as "historicity" or "historicality" and means "historical relevance, or authenticity." In order to clarify the way in which history can have personal, existential meaning, Bultmann and others have used *Geschichtlichkeit* to mean existential historicity in which people try to understand themselves as historical beings. In distinction from *Historie* as facts, and *Geschichte* as events, *Geschichtlichkeit* deals with events that have meaning toward me *now*.

All three of these specific German terms must be contained in an overview of reality as history, for they are different ways of looking at the general *historicity* of human beings and their world in order to understand its nature and meaning, and the way it functions in the search for a usable past. The same perspective can be used in discussing the question of tradition. Tradition understood in categories of *Historie* refers to the underlying facts that are reflected in the *traditions* of the church. These can only be discovered by means of careful historical criticism and the conclusions concerning the facts and their importance are always provisional. Tradition understood in categories of *Geschichte* refers to the original events and their meaning for the community of faith which shaped them into *Tradition*. This meaning again is ascertained through historical criticism and is open to reinterpretation. Yet the effort to know the original meaning of events in the tradition is crucial for seeking to interpret and reinterpret the sending action of God in other times and places. Tradition understood in categories of *Geschichtlichkeit* refers to tradition as a human existential for us today and includes the original facts and original meanings as they become our *tradition* which is used to shape our life and future.

In the light of our analysis we can see that the search for a usable history includes far more than critical research into the bare facts. Equally important is an investigation of who recorded the data; the meaning for those who recorded them; and the constantly changing existential meaning of this still living and evolving past. In a historicized world people are set free to shape themselves and their destiny in different ways, and it is just because of this that liberation theology takes on such an important meaning in today's world. Knowing that an unexamined history operates as fate, liberation theologians are trying to seek out the meaning of Christian tradition so that it speaks the good news of liberation in concrete circumstances of oppression and liberates the minds and actions of people. In the search into tradition and history it is necessary to operate at all three interlocking levels of investigation and interpretation in order to provide a way of escaping a fated world in which the future has been closed off by the established traditions of certain men. With these tools oppressed groups in church and society can seek to create a usable history that points toward the liberating power of the future.

Invisible Histories. The experience of Third World people and women is that they are frequently *invisible,* not only in today's society but also in history. In society the dominant decision makers are the ones who "count." They are usually listened to at social gatherings, meetings, and in the media. They are the writers of most history books and the recorders of their own important position. Women and other groups, however, are busy in the rewriting of history so that distortions are exposed and their own contributions to culture and society are made visible.

The invisibility of oppressed groups is apparent in church history and traditions as well as in other fields. Here, as is usually the case, history has been written by the *victors.* Those who lost the struggle for their points of view and for changes in the status quo were written out of the history of the church as heretics or schismatics. Those who shared in the struggles of the Christian people as women, by and large, remained invisible in an androcentric or male-dominated church and culture.

Yet as they search back into Biblical and ecclesiastical history women and other groups find more and more that they were not entirely invisible. Somehow the Tradition of God seems to have *broken through* the traditions of men to provide clues of the hidden presence of the oppressed and forgotten members of the human family. The Bible records a long and complex history of people's response to the God of their liberation.[22] The traditioning process itself, of interpretation and reinterpretation of the meaning of God's love and human obedience and response, can be seen taking place as the story of the Bible and of the Christian church unfolds.

In Old Testament research there is a constant attempt to discover the *Historie* which has become an invisible layer behind the *Geschichte* as it now stands. Of particular interest to women are the traditions of Canaanite religion as seen in such documents as the Ugaritic texts. The Yahwist conflict with the worship of fertility gods is one of the causes of the strongly defensive patriarchal tradition with its stress on male images of God. The Canaanite traditions often were challenged and destroyed or assimilated by the Hebrew traditions. This suggests the likelihood of the existence of elements from the Canaanite worship of the Mother Goddess which may have been incorporated into the Hebrew concept of God.[23]

Within the Biblical tradition itself it is also possible to perceive points at which God chooses to make women instruments of Tradition in breaking through the usually accepted roles women played in the Hebrew culture. Thus in pointing to the importance of Miriam, Deborah, and Huldah at key moments of Israel's history (Ex. 15:21; Judg. 4:4 ff.; II Kings 22:14), Samuel Terrien writes:

In the world of the Ancient Near East, where the fruitfulness of the soil, the fertility of animals, and a large progeny were associated as signs of divine blessings, woman was understandably considered primarily as a wife and a mother. Nevertheless, several women who left their mark in the religious life of the nation stood out on their own genius or achievement, and not in relation to husband, family or descendance.[24]

Such breakthroughs form an important part of *Geschicht-lichkeit* or still living and evolving tradition for women as they seek to share in the tasks of the church in the modern world.

The same sort of breakthroughs are to be seen in the New Testament especially in the Gospels and in the writings of Paul. Jesus lived as part of postexilic Jewish culture which had adopted a restricted view of the role and status of women, since the prohibitions against their participation in worship and in society begun after the Babylonian exile.[25] Yet he persisted in treating women as full persons. For Jesus, women, like the sick, the lame, the blind, and the sinners, were persons. To them *all* he offered a full place in God's Kingdom. He understood his ministry as bringing good news of liberation to *all* the oppressed (Matt. 11:2–6). In the story of Jesus and the Samaritan woman he is pictured talking in public with a woman when it was forbidden that Jewish men should speak in public to women or associate with Samaritans (John 4:7–30). It is clear that he allowed women to follow him as disciples and to support him in his ministry (Luke 8: 1–3). In spite of the disbelief of the "twelve," and a lack of legal qualification as witnesses, women were the first witnesses of the resurrection and handed on the Tradition to others (Luke 24:1–11).

Paul was also very much a part of the androcentric culture of his time, and his advice often reflected this particular situation. Yet exegesis shows that many of his supposedly sexist statements such as the one that says, "Women should keep silence in the churches," were not necessarily intended in the way they have been used in the Pastoral Epistles or church traditions (I Cor. 14:34). Paul's gospel messages were situation variable. In this sense they were *script*, not *Scripture*, and dealt with the problem at hand. His overriding concern was to preach the gospel so that it would be heard and not create a scandal. In spite of his injunctions to women to conform to the prevailing social and religious patterns, he still recognized that the Tradition was being handed over into the hands of both men and women (I Cor. 11:2–16). The "gifts of the Holy Spirit" were received by both women and men, and Paul encouraged both to preach, to pray, and to work as fellow apostles and servants in Christ (I Cor. 12: 6;14:26–36). For Paul the church was a sign of the New Age, begun in Jesus Christ and breaking into history, and he affirmed that its members should recognize no distinctions among themselves as Jew or Greek, slave or free, male or female (Gal. 3:28).

Historically, it seems that Paul's words to the Galatians were too radical for their time. As the church settled down to live in the existing social order, it became more and more concerned with order and authority, and less and less with freedom. Yet some of Paul's words and other teachings of the gospel had a revolutionary dynamic which was reflected in the openness of the early church toward woman's role. This dynamic keeps fermenting and breaking out in every age.[26]

It is to this breaking out of Tradition that liberation theology looks as it continues to research into the various struggles of groups often branded as heretics by the church. Attention is focused by women on the contribution of the Gnostics and the Montanists in the early centuries because of the equality and leadership of women in these groups, and their stress on the inclusion of the female attributes in the Godhead.[27] In the same way scholars are examining the role of the abbess as having "quasi-episcopal power" in the Middle Ages, and the contribution of women to the Reformation and to nineteenth-century missions.[28]

Other groups concerned with liberation and a usable past are doing the same type of research and reinterpretation in respect to traditions that are important to their own identity. They have rediscovered the Donatist controversy with Augustine in North Africa as an early social protest by the indigenous black population of Berbers (and possibly the Punic population) against the Romans and their church authority.[29] In the searching out of the histories of those who are oppressed, new heroes and heroines emerge. The work of

Thomas Müntzer of the left wing of the Reformation takes on new light. The various sects and independent churches both ancient and modern become an object of search into the nature of the liberating action of God's power in history.[30] It may be that this research into the history of the outcasts of society and "heretics" of the church will become the basis for new formulations of a *usable history*. Certainly the evidence of the revolutionary dynamic of liberation in all phases of history will help to strengthen those who look to the Tradition of God as the basis of their hope in action as they seek to shape a new future.

Myth and History. The examination of myth is an important part of building a usable future, for, as with history, unexamined myths operate as fate. In fact, one of the characteristics of myths is that they are a means of linking the present with the power and authority of the past in order to provide a human self-definition which legitimates the status quo. For liberation theologians, trying to set the minds and hearts of people free for shaping the future in new ways, myths are a key object of investigation. For women they take on even more importance because the relation of men and women in society is so basic that there is a great body of mythological material related to the social expectation of this relationship in various cultures.

Many myths represent false images of reality and need to be destroyed. Yet others can be helpful and need to be studied in order to relate them to a historical understanding of reality and to transmythologize their power into new frameworks of meaning. Although we live in a historicized and technological world which is primarily oriented toward the problems of shaping the future, myths still have an important place in our lives, not as *Historie* but as symbolic insights into the human condition. Thus Mircea Eliade points out that myths can supply models of meaning for human conduct and action.[31]

In "primitive" societies myth is "the primordial form of

the intellectual expression of religious beliefs and attitudes" according to Thomas O'Dea. "It is an emotion-laden assertion" of peoples' place in a world that is meaningful to them, and their solidarity with it.[32] *Mythologies* are used as self-definitions of a group living in close relation to a static, natural world with reference to the continuing power of its origins. In contrast, the *ideologies* of modern society are used as self-interpretations of a group which sees itself as part of a changing, historicized world. Karl Marx has pointed out that ideologies are ideas that can serve as tools for change because they expose the contradictions in the present society in order to move toward the desired future. Ideologies such as nationalism and socialism play an important part in the modern world because they help to explain and justify the course of transition and the goals involved in it.[33]

Ideologies, however partial or distorted in their description of reality, take on major importance in reference to social and political changes needed in today's world and in the writing of liberation theology. But myths cannot be ignored. They still have power in the minds of people because they continue to be part of the still living and evolving past in conscious and unconscious ways. In addition to this, religious myths form an important element in the description of God's traditioning action and of the relation of men and women to this action. As Bultmann and others have long since pointed out, much of the Biblical tradition is formed in a mythical thought world and needs to be understood by means of demythologizing and transmythologizing into historical categories.[34]

One type of myth that calls for constant attention by those concerned with Tradition is that of *etiologies* such as those contained in Gen., chs. 1 to 11. Even though the stories as they presently stand in Genesis have been historicized as the Primeval History of humankind, they still contain many of the original elements of etiological myths which tell the story of the origin of a people and their place in God's world.[35]

Such etiological myths come out of the collective consciousness of a people, and it is not possible, simply by sitting down and writing, to create new ones that bring with them the power and meaning of the original myths. It is not possible because our present world does not have a collective consciousness that expresses itself in this "primitive" form of self-definition. Although basic psychological archetypes may continue in our unconscious we do not live in a world that primarily explains its origins through myth.

Nevertheless, the etiological myths contained in Genesis continue to express theological truths which have meaning to those who live by the Tradition of God. As presently cast they speak of the experience of the world and its creation from the perspective of the saving acts of liberation through which Israel has experienced God in the exodus.[36] The *Geschichte* continues to point to the deep meaning felt in the relation of Israel and of the whole of creation to the God of their deliverance, even though the interpretation of that story in terms of *Geschichtlichkeit* changes for us as we try to understand it in our own situation. As new discoveries in archaeology, manuscripts, and traditions add new light to the *Historie* reflected in the texts, this aids us in our search and interpretation of these powerful myths. For this reason historical tools of critical research continue to be important tools of "iconoclasm turned backward" in order to continue in the search for meaning in traditions that relate to our own lives.

Attempts to transmythologize such myths by introducing new mythical materials from either later or pre-Biblical sources present some problems for Biblically based theology. Such attempts as Theodor Reik's description of the creation of Eve as a primal version of the circumcision rite in which Adam is reborn, or the use of the legend of the powerful "Lilith" to show that Eve was Adam's second wife, do not appear to increase the power and beauty of the story as it is now told by the Yahwist.[37] At best they play the role of new ideologies that counteract, not the original meaning, but the way the story has been interpreted in Hebrew and Christian traditions. These new forms of myth serve to excite the imagination, to raise questions, and to provide countermyths which may be useful for desired changes in current society, but they tend to miss the deep theological meanings already present in the story which point to the partnership of man and woman in God's creation.[38]

Another type of myth that is present in our world today is the *common social myth*. This type reflects the institutionalization of prejudice in such a way that this "folk wisdom" serves to reinforce the status quo.[39] These social myths need to be exposed as false where they are seen to be false and alienating to the self-definition of any group in society. As Paulo Freire points out, these myths have to be "demystified" and exposed rather than transmythologized or interpreted into a new form.[40] An obvious way to do this is by means of *Historie*—telling the real facts of the case. Facts must be used to counter false social myths such as: "All poor are lazy." "Blacks have small brains." "Women are a bad risk in careers or professional employment." "The children of women who work will suffer."[41]

"Facts," however, do not always eliminate the social myths or illusions as long as the social structures which they express remain, so it is important to use other strategies as well. One is the creation of countermyths or slogans that capture the minds of people intent for change. "Woman is not 'the Other,' she is 'the partner.' "[42] "Beyond 'the battle of the sexes' to 'complementarity.' " "Sisterhood is powerful."[43] Another means used by some people to expose the absurdity of social myths is to act out those absurdities in groups called "WITCH" and Black Panthers, etc. But the myths ultimately change only through social and political changes which remove the inequalities that have been legitimatized by the old myths.

However we approach the difficult and complicated issue

of myths in religion and society, it is important to remember that they continue to have subconscious power as a still living and evolving past in our lives and consequently need to be treated with critical respect.[44] They contain elements of both useless and usable history. The ability to distinguish between these two pasts and to deal with them creatively in the consciousness and actions of people is an important ingredient in the search for human liberation in today's world.

USABLE LANGUAGE

As human beings we make use of language to communicate our thoughts, emotions, and actions. Our use of language is a vital means of participation in God's Mission of handing over Christ into the hands of all generations and nations *(Tradition)*. Yet the language at our disposal frequently presents problems of communication, creating situations more like the story of Babel than of Pentecost. The symbols and words of church *traditions* have become so encrusted by their formation in a sexist and racist Western culture that the language sometimes becomes a barrier to communication. For those who experience the barriers of exclusion on the basis of racial or biological origin, the past becomes useless when language, as well as history and myth, is used to reinforce these patterns of prejudice. The message of God's love is thus effectively blocked because it ceases to be part of a still living and evolving *tradition* in their conscious perception of themselves and the world in which they live.

Generic Nonsense. To counteract this, many Third World groups are turning to the traditions, languages, and dialects of their own culture as a medium of expression which specifically includes their own life experience. The same process is going on in the movement for women's liberation where the problem of "desexing language" has taken on particular importance. In North America women are seeking to find *hu-*

man pronouns which clearly interpret the fact that *both* men and women are included in the words expressed.[45] The English usage of such words as man, men, his, mankind, brotherhood, etc., *in the generic sense* has been increasingly called into question. However much a particular person or organization may protest that the words *really mean* human, human beings, his and hers, humankind, peoplehood, etc., the fact remains that women are frequently left out of both the mental structures and the social structures of our culture. Their history is not only invisible, they themselves are frequently invisible in the way the male-dominated society speaks its language and makes its decisions. Thus in speaking of consciousness-raising and male language structure, Nelle Morton says:

As women questioned the generic use of male words they were promptly put down repeatedly with ridicule. Finally it became quite evident to them that male and not the generic in the male terminology was meant.[46]

Those who say that this concern of women for language that is whole, positive, and inclusive is unreasonable should begin to think about what it is like to sit through years of lectures, sermons, instructions, etc., in which one is never named, even by inclusion in the pronouns used. This experience of being kept in her "invisible place" is a constant reality for a woman both in church and in society. In describing the result of such experience of discrimination and the consequent loss of identity or growth of self-conscious rage, Simone de Beauvoir says:

It is, in point of fact, a difficult matter for man to realize the extreme importance of social discriminations which seem outwardly insignificant but which produce in woman moral and intellectual effects so profound that they appear to spring from her original nature.[47]

The way people use language reflects the images in their lives and the patterns of their social behavior. As social patterns and images in church and society change this may have an effect on our language so that it becomes more inclusive of those who find themselves "left out." One way to help such changes to come about is to begin *now* by taking the trouble to include others in the way we speak by changing our own linguistic models.

Nowhere is woman's experience of male-dominated language more pervasive than in the church and synagogue. Such "he" language is applied "in the generic sense" to God, to the preacher, to the worshiper. In hymns, liturgies, and styles of government, religious life is male-oriented. It is *generic nonsense* to say that women are included linguistically when they are excluded by so many practices. If this is to change, the Biblical, theological, and ecclesial traditions must be interpreted and translated so that the liberating power of God's love can break through in new words and actions. The search for a usable past includes the search for usable language and new forms of expression. In a theology of liberation this search begins through the interpretation of Tradition as it is recorded in the Biblical experience and an examination of the names we use to refer to God.

When we examine the Biblical language that describes God's purpose of handing over Jesus Christ into the hands of women and men we are confronted not only with exegetical but also with *hermeneutical* problems. Exegesis can help us examine the *Historie* and *Geschichte* so that we know as much as possible about the *facts* of the situation and the *factors* that were considered of importance in the community that shaped a particular Biblical tradition. Krister Stendahl has pointed out, however, that the hermeneutical principles of application and interpretation are not settled by the exegesis.[48] In the history of the church certain facts and meanings have tended to be ignored while others, emphasized as the *Geschichte*, become *Geschichtlichkeit* in human experience. For instance, the injunction of Jesus to his disciples to walk staff in hand is largely ignored while his sayings on divorce have been interpreted in a legalistic fashion.[49] To deal faithfully with the Scriptures, it is necessary to be conscious of the way in which the events have been interpreted in various cultural contexts, not only to understand these developments but also to make clear the importance of continued interpretation that helps the gospel message become "good news" in present society.

The Freedom of God. We have seen that some of the perspectives of liberation theologies are: Biblical promise; world as history; and salvation as a social event. These perspectives lead theologians to emphasize the liberating power of God through language that points to God's freedom. God is *free from* manipulation of any one group as their private "Baal"; yet God chooses to be *free for* all humanity in order to open up "a future and a hope" (Jer. 29:11). The liberating purpose of God in history is reflected in the theological understanding of the *economic Trinity.* The Bible witnesses to the Mission of God as an economy of salvation.[50] God's dealings with humanity are spoken of as *oikonomia* (stewardship, economy) for the *oikoumenē* (world). In these dealings God is revealed as Creator, Liberator, and Reconciler.[51] Throughout the Biblical tradition the descriptions of God's actions and the metaphorical names and images used of God reveal a deep awareness of the transcendence of God. God's reality is a mystery that cannot be described except insofar as that mystery is seen through God's salvific activity in history. This self-revelation signifies not only God's freedom from all creation but also God's freedom to suffer with women and men in their groaning for full human liberation. As Moltmann points out, God's transcendence can be described in historical metaphors which point to the future as the "coming of God."[52] In this *"metachronical"* (as distinct from *metaphysical*) way of speaking, God transcends us as our future; God is coming toward us *(adventus).* "*God is* present in the way in which . . . [God's] future takes control over the present in real anticipations and prefigurations. *But God is not as yet* present in the form of . . . [God's] eternal presence."[53]

The key passage that speaks of the freedom of God in relation to the naming of God is Ex. 3:13–21.[54] This difficult passage shows great reticence about the name of God. Von Rad tells us that,

according to ancient ideas, a name was not just "noise and smoke": instead, there was a close and essential relationship between it and its subject. The subject is in the name, and on that account the name carries with it a statement about the nature of its subject or at least about the power appertaining to it.[55]

It is small wonder then that Moses asks to know the name of God. The answer is an act of "self-presentation." A probable descriptive translation of the mysterious words in v. 14 might well be "I cause to happen, what will happen."[56] To explain this eventful God, vs. 15 and following speak of Yahweh as the God of Abraham, Isaac, and Jacob who will be the God of liberation for the chosen people, in affliction and distress.[57] This is the divine self God presents: free *from* all human restrictions; free to happen for humankind.[58] Yahweh is seen as a "happening" God of past, present, and future.

In speaking of God's *oikonomia* we are describing the way God chooses to be *with us*. When we move beyond this historical, descriptive language to metaphors about God's reality, it is important not to confuse the metaphor with the reality itself. There is an ancient Zen saying which is a helpful reminder to all those who would use their *logos* in reflecting on God's actions:

The finger points to the moon and woe is the one who confuses the finger with the moon!

God language should not be confused with the reality of God, but should struggle to disclose that reality through careful investigation and interpretation.

Forgotten Names of God. However we choose to describe God's transcendence, the mystery of God's freedom points to a reality that is clearly beyond both *biological* distinctions of male and female and *cultural* distinctions of masculine and feminine. The metaphors used in our language about God are rooted in human experience. In this sense all the cultural characteristics that are used to describe masculine and feminine qualities can be used in speaking of God as a means of reflecting the totality of human experience. In the androcentric cultures of the Biblical traditions masculine characteristics are most frequently ascribed to God as a projection of male authority and superiority in the societies.

In its continuous confrontation with Canaanite polytheism in which male deities often had female counterparts, Israel tried to concentrate all divine functions and roles into one God. In the course of history the earlier traditions, that ascribed to Yahweh the characteristics of both male and female deities *(elohim)*, tended to be replaced by only masculine features. This antifeminine bias probably increased in post-Babylonian traditions which considered women "ritually unclean."[59] Until recently little attention has been paid to the way androcentric Biblical and church traditions have affected the editing, translation, and interpretation of texts. Now women are beginning to raise questions in this area as they search for the many *forgotten names of God.* Even in their present form, the Biblical and ecclesial traditions reveal some characteristics of God which were and still are considered to be feminine.

The passage in Ex., ch. 3, describing God's self-revelation to Moses points toward an image of God that is sometimes overlooked in our view of Old Testament tradition: the image of *servant.* In and through the actions of the liberator are those of the servant or helper *('ezer).* The Ex. 34:6 interpretation of the name Yahweh makes this more clear as it reminds us that "God is merciful and gracious, slow to anger and abounding in steadfast love and faithfulness."[60] Yahweh is related to humankind in a covenant relationship of love and concern.

This same idea is reflected in the two Genesis versions of

creation. Genesis 1:26 speaks of the creation of man and woman in the image of God. "Let us make . . . [humankind] in our image, after our likeness; and let them have dominion over . . . all the earth." "Male and female . . . [God] created them." Exactly what the author means by the word "image" is not clear, but it is evident that the Priestly writer wishes to point to an analogy between God and man-and-woman. The analogy is not merely *anthropomorphic* because in Israel's view human beings are *theomorphic*.[61] They are an image of *Elohim*. The plural word for God *(Elohim)* and the words "let us . . ." reflect not only the idea of God surrounded by a heavenly court but also the notion of God as combining all the characteristics of the male and female gods in the Canaanite pantheon which Yahweh now transcends, yet includes.[62] The most important aspects of the image which humanity bears are the close relationship of love between themselves and God and the responsibility given them as God's representatives to care for the rest of creation as God's helpers.[63] The word "dominion" does not necessarily imply that humankind is to destroy or exploit nature, but man and woman are to be held responsible before God for the way they serve God in taking care of the world.

God's characteristic as servant is even more clear in the Gen., ch. 2, description. Here as the climax of the creation story Eve is created as the helper *('ezer)* of Adam.[64] Along with other scholars Samuel Terrien has indicated that

. . . woman is created as help and succor to man's loneliness. Far from denoting the idea of service in a subordinated position, the word "help" *('ezer)* is generally applied to God who is par excellence the succor of those in need and in despair. Woman is not a mere tool of physiological or psychological delight. She fulfills a function of creative complementariness.[65]

Here we see again that the image of God as servant and helper is reflected in the way that humanity is to be of mutual help and obedience.

This image of God as servant emerges clearly in the New Testament in the figure of Jesus, who came "not to be served but to serve" (Mark 10:45). Jesus of Nazareth was identified with the prophecies of God's "suffering servant" (Isa. 42:1–4). Above all, he became God's instrument of divine help in his refusal to crave "equality with God" and willingness to live among people in self-surrender to others in love (Phil. 2: 5–11).[66]

From this brief analysis we can conclude that it is not necessary to think of God primarily as having masculine characteristics of domination and lordship, a practice that has served to legitimate aggression and domination in androcentric cultures. It is also possible to think of God as having characteristics frequently thought of as feminine. God extends divine help to those in need through the chosen instruments. The example of the steadfast love and sacrifice of God in the Old and New Testaments points to possibilities of a world where the fullness of these characteristics could be displayed by both men and women.

Another forgotten name or image of God which mirrors the cultural and biological role of women is seen in the use of *bird imagery* in the Scriptures. Here God's concern for humanity is expressed in imagery that possibly is drawn from the representation of female goddesses with *sheltering wings.*[67] Yahweh is described by an analogy to the action of a female bird protecting her young (Ps. 17:8; 36:7; 57:1; 91: 1,4; Isa. 31:5; etc.). The sustaining care of Yahweh for Israel is represented in Deut. 32:11–12 by the words: "Like an eagle that stirs up its nest, that flutters over its young, spreading out its wings, catching them, bearing them on its pinions, the LORD alone did lead him, and there was no foreign god with him." In a similar reference in Matt. 23:37 (Luke 13:34) Jesus says: "O Jerusalem, Jerusalem . . . ! How often would I have gathered your children together as a hen gathers her brood under her wings, and you would not!" The Bible also contains winged figures of women referring to divine visions in a way similar to that of Eastern folk tales (Zech. 5:9; Rev. 12:14).[68]

These lead us to consider specific images or names of God as *mother* or *wife.* This image is not always used to apply to Israel or the church as the wife. Sometimes the roles are reversed as in Ps. 51. Terrien points out that here the poet

. . . throws himself upon God's pardon by crying out, "Have mercy upon me, O God, on account of thy motherly compassions" (*rachamim,* plural of majesty of *rechem,* "uterus"). It is probable that the verb itself, *chanan,* from which derives the noun *chen,* "grace," meant originally "to long for" in the sense of maternal instinct.[69]

Other passages compare the love of God with the love of a mother for her child, or the loyalty and affection of a wife for her husband (Deut. 32:18; Isa. 46:3; 51:1; 49:14–15; Ps. 131: 2).[70]

Lastly we need to remind ourselves of the importance of three words used in the femine gender in Hebrew tradition which stress feminine attributes of God: Shekinah or the glory of the presence of God on earth; Torah or the guidance of God; Chokmah or the pre-cosmic divine wisdom.[71] In the New Testament, Jesus is associated with all three of these attributes, according to W. D. Davies.

Thus in Matt. 18:20 we read: "For where two or three are gathered together in my name, there am I in the midst of them." With this we may compare the saying in *Pirke Aboth:* "When they sit together and are occupied with the Torah, the Shekinah is among them."[72]

In I Cor. 1:24, 30, Paul calls Christ the Wisdom of God.[73] From this we can conclude that both feminine and masculine characteristics play a part in the description of Yahweh and Christ.

The same can also be said of the Spirit which is spoken of in Hebrew by a word of feminine gender, *ruach* ("wind" or "breath"), and translated into Greek in the neuter gender as *pneuma.*[74] The functions of the Holy Spirit as characterized in Biblical texts are often, but not exclusively, those which have been associated with women: consolation, eschatological groaning in travail of childbirth, emotional warmth, and inspiration. In addition, André Dumas has pointed out that some of the ancient church traditions refer to the Holy Spirit in feminine rather than masculine terms. "Syriac theology (and sometimes Orthodox Theology) often regarded it as an archetype of femininity and hypostatic union."[75]

By their nature and work all three Persons of the Trinity transcend the categories of masculine and feminine, yet the human metaphors used to speak of all three of them include human characteristics of all types. Even the *immanent Trinity* which is the theological way of speaking about the relation of the "persons" of the Trinity among themselves can be said to transcend, and also to include, all the characteristics familiar to us by analogy to human love.[76] Because of experience of God's self-communication to the world in the work of the *economic Trinity,* it is possible to affirm the immanent nature of the Trinity as a dynamic communication of love between the "persons" of the Trinity. In spite of their distinction of function the Creator, Liberator, and Comforter share in one divine communication of love to humanity which is experienced in different ways.

In the light of the necessity of making clear that the Tradition is for *all* and not for just one half of humanity, it is perhaps wise to revise our language in speaking of God. For instance, it is possible to speak of God the Creator without using male pronouns, as an indication that God transcends all biological and cultural distinctions of sex. This sometimes makes a sentence more difficult, but it allows our language of God to be heard more clearly by *both* men and women. In the same way we can emphasize the role of Christ the Liberator and Redeemer as one that represents God's freedom to be present with all humanity *(Emmanuel).* In order to make clear the fact that the metaphors for the Godhead include those which are both masculine and feminine, it is perhaps also helpful at this moment in history to speak of the Holy Spirit, the Comforter and Reconciler, with a feminine pronoun.

Above all, in the search for *the usable past* it is important to maintain the dynamic of God's Tradition by speaking and acting in such ways that all people can find for themselves a place in that Tradition by perceiving that God offers to them a *usable future,* a *usable history,* and a *usable language.* In this way the reality of God's handing over Jesus Christ into the hands of all generations and nations can be seen as a still living and evolving past with which to shape the future in community with others today. The heresy of our time is not that of reexamining the Biblical and ecclesial traditions. It is the refusal of the church to hear the cry of oppressed people, and to speak and act on behalf of liberation for all.[77] This is the challenge we face, for, as Terrien says:

Many questions . . . remain for contemporary theologians to investigate. Biblical faith, however, from Abraham to Jesus Christ, lays the basis of a theology of womanhood [and manhood] which goes counter to the traditional attitudes and practices of Christendom and challenges the church of today to re-think critically and creatively the respective functions of man and woman.[78]

4: SALVATION
AND CONSCIENTIZATION

Liberation theology brings into focus the Biblical message of God's Mission to set humankind free from bondage. In the light of oppression experienced by Third World people and women, it seeks to tell the good news of liberation in such a way that people can hear, understand, and accept this message of God's gift of freedom and salvation in their lives. The "cantus firmus of the liberating message" of the Bible is the good news *(basar)* of deliverance experienced by the Hebrew people, and the good news *(euangelion)* of the establishment of God's rulership as experienced by the early followers of Jesus Christ (Isa. 52:7; Matt. 4:17).[1] These acts of deliverance are also the basis of traditioning into the present experience and future hope of those who seek liberation *now*.

Those who would participate in God's Tradition by handing over Jesus Christ to others must, themselves, accept the challenge that these situations of oppression present to the way in which we have understood and interpreted God's will for salvation of all humankind. This challenge to interpret the meaning of salvation today calls for a praxis methodology. Not only must we reflect on the meaning of God's actions of *salvation as liberation* in the Biblical context, but also we must relate this action to the experience of freedom which happens as *conscientization and liberation* among oppressed people. For God's traditioning action is also to be seen in and through the recognition of a still living and evolving past that calls for commitment to shape the future. The examination of the human experience of conscientization then leads us to look at its relation to the divine-human experience of *conversion and evangelism.*

SALVATION AS LIBERATION

For Christians all over the world a deep concern has long been felt to express the meaning of salvation in terms that can be heard by people within various cultural situations and different confessional backgrounds.[2] The task has become especially urgent in the face of modern secular thinking which focuses on the need for social change and the shaping of society here and now, rather than on the need for an individualized afterlife.

This concern is reflected in the investigations and meetings of the World Council of Churches. In the 1963 Mexico City conference of the Division of World Mission and Evangelism the question was posed: "What is the content of the salvation, the rescue, the emancipation which Jesus Christ offers to secularized . . . [people] in this era?"[3] The next world conference in Bangkok (1973) sought to follow through on this question by a multifaceted investigation of "Salvation Today." It brought together people from all the six continents to share their experiences as Christians and non-Christians of the meaning of salvation today, and to ask how the Bible and traditions speak to these experiences.[4] This same area of investigation is to be seen in the theme of the 1975 World Council Assembly, which will meet in Djakarta to discuss how "Jesus Christ Frees and Unites."

Without minimizing the many differences of approach, theology, and situation that are involved in any discussion of the meaning of salvation, we would note that one of the recurring themes which emerged in the preparation and discussion of these world meetings was that *salvation today* has to do with *liberation now* from all those things which keep humanity in slavery.[5]

The message of salvation as expressed in the Bible and heard among the nations today cannot be reduced to one simple formula. It is not simply focused on "individual salvation," nor on "social salvation."[6] This gift of the liberating power of God's love is experienced in different situations and times, in various ways. Yet, in spite of the situation variability of its description, it is clear that salvation has to do with new joy and wholeness, freedom and hope that is experienced in the lives of individuals and communities as a gift of God. This message of liberation is good news to those of our age who are searching for freedom, for meaning, for community, for authentic existence as human beings.[7] Before we look more closely at this contemporary experience, however, we need to look at the way salvation was understood in other ages and how it speaks to us today in the incessant cry of the peoples of the earth to be set free.

Shalom: Liberation and Blessing. One of the problems that Christians face in bridging their theological differences is that there is often a confusion in the meaning and traditions of certain words. One of these English words is *salvation.* The confusion about salvation contributes to a polarization between the conservatives ("evangelicals") and the social activists ("ecumenicals"). This dichotomy can be seen in the meetings of denominations as well as in National Council or World Council meetings.[8]

In the Old Testament there is no one "doctrine" of salvation and words such as "to deliver" *(hoshia')* and "to redeem" *(ga'al)* are used to describe what God has done and will do for the Hebrew people. One of the most important words for the goal of salvation is *shalom.*[9] This word has a wide spectrum of meanings which include, not only peace but also personal, familial, and social wholeness, well-being, and prosperity. Johannes Pedersen describes *shalom* as

... the most comprehensive denomination of happiness, as it designates the healthy development in all forms, both of the harmony within the covenant and all progress in life.[10]

Shalom is a social event, a venture in co-humanity which cannot be reduced to a formula. The word itself represents a summary of all the gifts that God promises to humanity; the fulfillment of God's intention for all creation. This promise is to be fulfilled in the coming of the Prince of Peace to "establish it ... with justice and with righteousness" (Isa. 9:6–7). It is described in Ps. 85:8–13 as a gift of salvation to God's people in which all the promises of God will be fulfilled:

Steadfast love and faithfulness will meet;
 righteousness and peace *(shalom)* will kiss each other.
Faithfulness will spring up from the ground,
 and righteousness will look down from the sky.
Yea, the LORD will give what is good,
 and our land will yield its increase.

In the Old Testament two of the key motifs of salvation overlap or converge in the meaning of *shalom*. These two motifs have been identified by Claus Westermann as liberation and blessing.[11] The first motif of *liberation* refers to deliverance from suffering, distress, death, sin, anxiety, pursuit, and imprisonment. From the time of the exodus onward Yahweh is portrayed as a liberating God who sets the people free. The nature of God who "happens" in actions of liberation enables the people to continue to hope for and expect this deliverance to happen again in history.

The second motif is that of *blessing*. God as Creator and sustainer of humanity is seen as the one who blessed creation and declared that "it was very good" (Gen. 1:28, 31). This motif of blessing appears especially in the stories of the Patriarchs and in Deuteronomy (Gen. 12:1–3; Deut. 28:3–6).[12] The result of God's blessing, given to Abraham, and handed down from father to son, was the inner strength of soul (as total spiritual and physical being) and the happiness it created. God's blessing brings fertility in family and in the field, as well as victory over all enemies.[13] The blessing is the power of life which creates wholeness and goodness in both creature and creation. The word *shalom* includes this totality of blessing as a description of the goal of God's liberating action as a past event and a promised hope.

In the Gospels the two overlapping motifs of *shalom* appear in the One who came as the Prince of Shalom to fulfill the Messianic promise of salvation (Luke 2:14; John 14:27). In the Sermon on the Mount we see that those who choose to accept the rulership of God as announced and represented in Jesus of Nazareth are blessed (Matt. 5:1–11). And in Christ they experience the reality and promise of deliverance and redemption (Matt. 1:21; 10:22; 19:25). Jesus embodies the meaning of *shalom* through his acts of healing (blessing), as well as his action of crucifixion and resurrection (liberation).

In Paul's writings and in the later epistles, however, the word most often used to connote salvation, *sōtēria*, is reduced from the wider spectrum of *shalom* and deals mainly with the divine-human relationship and not with social relationships. Paul speaks of *sōtēria* in three different ways: as a once and for all occurrence in Jesus Christ, as an ongoing process in our lives, as a future realization.[14]

As we move into the early period of church history we discover a tendency to reduce and narrow the broader understanding of *shalom* even farther in the light of the Hellenistic view of the separation of body and soul. The Latin word *salus*, used to translate the word *sōtēria*, became focused even more clearly on one aspect of liberation—that of the eternal destiny of the soul in the afterlife. This *salus* was to be mediated by the church.[15]

This description of the narrowing of the meaning of *shalom* as blessing and liberation is only one part of what has happened to our understanding of salvation, but it helps to clarify the variety of approaches to salvation in the modern world, and their bases in the development of the traditions.

The same reduction can be seen in the understanding of sin in relation to *shalom.*

In the context of *shalom* and Israel's covenant of blessing and liberation, sin is understood as a breakdown of the covenant relationship caused by disobedience.[16] Frequent words for sin are *chatta'th* (missing the mark), *pesha'*(rebellion or violating the covenant), and *'awon* (disobedience).[17] In speaking of the "new covenant with the house of Israel and the house of Judah" Jeremiah's oracle says, "For I will forgive their iniquity *('awon)*, and I will remember their sin *(chatta'th)* no more" (Jer. 31:34). All three of the above terms are sometimes combined in one verse, as in Ex. 34:7 and Ps. 32:5.

Sin in the context of *sōtēria* in the New Testament is often focused on the lack of faith. One misses the mark *(hamartia)* by refusing to have a relationship of trust with God in Jesus Christ. Sin is viewed as "hatred of God" and rejection of Jesus Christ (Rom. 8:7; 14:23).[18] In the later church traditions, sin *(peccatum)* takes on a quantitative aspect in relation to the overcoming of sins through participation in the life of the church. Here it is understood more as the opposite of virtue rather than of faith or covenant relationship.[19]

These differences in the semantic spectrum of salvation and sin often lead to misunderstanding when we try to spell them out in various languages and traditions. Yet the historical character of salvation means that there have been and will be many changes in the interpretation of salvation and sin in different life situations.

Salvation Today. One of the interesting things that has happened to the understanding of salvation today is that, in a world of diversity and change, people feel free to use a variety of definitions of salvation. In the search for meaning every religion and ideology is explored for its offer of liberation, wholeness, and blessing.[20] There is a growing awareness of the wholeness of human beings in their body, mind, and spirit and in their social relationship in today's world. For some this has led to a renewed stress on *shalom* as a gift of total wholeness and well-being in community.[21] The search for peace in a wartorn world where each new outbreak of fighting brings not only untold suffering but the threat of total destruction has led others to speak of *shalom* as the symbol of peace and harmony for which they long and work. Others see *shalom* as an expression of wholeness and harmony between humanity and the environment which is being destroyed by a technological society.[22]

Nowhere is the stress on salvation as seen in the motifs of *shalom* clearer than among those searching for ways of expressing the good news of God's traditioning action in situations of oppression, hunger, and alienation in our sorry world. Liberation theologies, which seek to reflect on the praxis of God's liberation in the light of particular circumstances of oppression, are returning to the motifs of liberation and blessing as they are found in the Biblical tradition. Without denying that salvation includes the message of individual deliverance from sin and death (Rom., chs. 5 to 7) they, nevertheless, place emphasis on the total goal of salvation (Rom., ch. 8) which is the gift of *shalom* (complete social and physical wholeness and harmony). Gutiérrez says:

Salvation is not something otherworldly, in regard to which the present life is merely a test. Salvation—the communion of . . . [people] with God and the communion of . . . [people] among themselves—is something which embraces all human reality, transforms it, and leads it to its fullness in Christ.[23]

In these emerging liberation theologies the two overlapping motifs of *shalom* appear again as a description of the usable future. The first motif of *liberation* is seen as the gift of God's action in history, as well as the agenda of those who join together in community to transform the world. For Third World and Fourth World people the motif of liberation expresses an important aspect of the *shalom* for which they seek. Speaking about "The Dialectic of Theology and Life," James Cone reminds us that "Jesus is not a doctrine" but an eternal event of liberation who makes freedom possible. From this context of Christ as Liberator emerges a life of interdependence in the lives of black people. He is the Word of truth in their lives.[24] In the area of justice and economic development, those at work to bring about an evolutionary process for transforming economic, social, political, and mental structures point to a connection with salvation in its implication of freedom. Thus in *Liberation, Development and Salvation,* René Laurentin says that "development presupposes a liberation from systems in which any development is impossible."[25]

Writers such as Rosemary Ruether and Dorothee Sölle emphasize the same theme. Ruether, in her book *Liberation Theology,* speaks of the destructive character of dualisms such as that between the individual and the collective, and the body and the soul, and sets out to analyze various polarities which are barriers to the theology and praxis of liberation. Sölle speaks of the gospel's business as "liberation of all human beings. Its concern rests with the oppressed, the poor, the crying."[26]

The second motif that overlaps with liberation is the meaning and experience of *shalom* as *blessing.* In the writers concerned with liberation theology this is usually interpreted as *humanization:* the setting free of all humanity to have a future and a hope. The blessings of the Patriarchs are now interpreted in modern contexts as the need for full personal and social well-being, as well as the need for the power to participate in shaping the world.

For those who experience *shalom* as new wholeness and liberation as human beings, *sin* is also viewed as a collective reality. The social as well as the individual responsibility for sin is stressed so that *oppression* is itself viewed as a symbol of the social reality of sin. Dorothee Sölle writes:

Sin to us is eminently political, a social term: the sins of which Jesus reminds me and which he puts before my eyes are the sins of my own people, of my own white race, of my own bourgeois and propertied class.[27]

Going back to the root meaning of one word for salvation, (*yeshu'ah*, from a root meaning "to be broad, or spacious"; "to have room"), sin is interpreted as the denial of this room or space in which to live.[28] Just as Isa. 49:19–20 symbolizes the oppression of Israel as a land "too narrow for your inhabitants" and Ps. 4:1 speaks of salvation as the gift of "room when I was in distress," liberation theologies point to sin as the refusal to give others room to breathe and live as human beings. According to Gutiérrez,

Sin is regarded as a social, historical fact, the absence of . . . [humanhood] and love in relationships among . . . [people], the breach of friendship with God and with other . . . [people], and, therefore, an interior, personal fracture. When it is considered in this way, the collective dimensions of sin are rediscovered.[29]

Women are very much interested in the reinterpretation of the meaning of sin in a feminist perspective. In church traditions sin has been interpreted not only individualistically but also as associated with sex and with women. A forthright rejection of such misogyny, including the misinterpretations of the Adam and Eve story which flow from this perspective can be seen in many feminist writers. For instance, Mary Daly writes:

In the mentality of the Fathers, woman and sexuality were identified. Their horror of sex was also a horror of woman. There is no evidence that they realized the projected mechanisms involved in this misogynistic attitude. In fact, male guilt feelings over sex and hyper-susceptibility to sexual stimulation and suggestion were transferred to "the other," the guilty sex.[30]

Another area of reinterpretation of the traditions concerning sin which interests feminist writers is the male perspective on what constitutes human sin and temptation. Aggression, lust, and hybris may not be at the top of the list for women who have been enculturated to be submissive. Valarie Saiving Goldstein writes:

. . . the temptations of woman *as woman* are not the same as the temptations of man *as man*, and the specifically feminine forms of sin—"feminine" not because they are confined to women or because women are incapable of sinning in other ways but because they are outgrowths of the basic feminine character structure—have a quality which can never be encompassed by such terms as "pride," and "will-to-power." They are better suggested by such items as triviality, distractibility, and diffuseness; lack of an organizing center or focus; dependence on others for one's own self-definition; tolerance at the expense of standards of excellence . . . in short, underdevelopment or negation of self.[31]

In various liberation theologies sin is viewed not only as the opposite of liberation or the oppression of others but also as the opposite of humanization or the *dehumanization* of others by means of excluding their perspectives from the meaning of human reality and wholeness.

In summary we can say that salvation today, as well as the understanding of sin today, has regained its social and communal emphasis in writings on liberation theology. Not denying individual responsibility and accountability, they still drive us also to see the dimension of responsibility and accountability in terms of the liberation and blessing for all oppressed and defuturized persons. For many people today, liberation is understood as a gift of God at once personal and social which is only ours as it is constantly shared with others.

CONSCIENTIZATION AND LIBERATION

In our discussion of the search for a usable past we analyzed the importance of tradition, history, and language as a dynamic at work in the process of liberation. This dynamic is experienced in human communities as a *process of conscientization:* "the process by which men and women are awakened to their sociocultural reality, move beyond the alienations and constraints to which they are subjected, and affirm themselves as the conscious subjects and creators of their own historical future."[32] Such a process of cultural action is reflected in the Biblical description of people's historical response to God's traditioning action. It also can be seen in the way in which human beings come to an understanding of themselves and their world as a meaningful process.

In a dynamic situation of cultural change people move to new awareness of their place in history and their ability to define that place for themselves as they search for "room to breathe." At the same time the process of new awareness is experienced in the individual lives of women and men as a *dialectic of liberation* in which their own inner perceptions begin to reveal a new vision of themselves and others as whole persons.

Process of Conscientization. It is no surprise to those who are involved in the search for liberation from forms of oppression which close off life and future that conscientization is an important theme of liberation theologies. Although this word is most popular in Latin-American theology, it is widely used today as a "passport description" of one of the roads toward freedom. The impact of being "dragged into history" through the global phenomena of development and communications technology has led men and women in every society to become increasingly aware of the dehumanizing factors in their own lives. The oppressed begin to hope for a world where people have goods and home, and opportunity to shape their own futures. They begin to speak of political and social changes needed to bring justice, equality, and dignity. They begin the process of liberation by negating the negative of the present situation. The discovery that they can participate in creating a different future sets people free to search for the meaning of their own humanity.

Conscientization is descriptive of the same phenomenon as *consciousness-raising*, yet it emphasizes two additional important elements. First, it is viewed as an intentional action-education process which Freire describes as *cultural action.* "It is the way we culturally attack culture. It means to see culture always as a problem and not to let it become static, becoming a myth and mystifying us."[33] Second, conscientization is viewed as a continuing process which includes praxis (action-reflection). It is the interrelation of self-awareness which leads to action and action which leads to new awareness which constitutes a "permanent, constant dynamic of our attitude toward culture itself."[34] Freire has described the dynamic process of conscientization in a typology of stages of historical awareness and action: *doxa, logos, praxis, utopia.*

Similar typologies of the stages of human thought have been used as a means of analyzing what happens in the process of historicizing and, consequently secularizing our world view. In this process, mental structures are developed by which people learn to make sense of the changing, secular world by accepting history as the field of self-explanation of life.[35]

For instance, Cornelis van Peursen describes the stages of human thought as: mythical, ontological, and functional. In the *mythical* stage of "primitive" society the subject is merged with the object and the human being is a dependent part of nature. In the *ontological* stage the subject and object are separate and the human being searches for existence perceived as separate from self, and divides the world into nature and supernature (metaphysics). In the *functional* stage of secular society the subject and object are perceived as functionally related and things do not exist in themselves, but for the sake of what they do to human beings.[36] All of these stages of thought exist in the world today and perhaps, to some extent, in the life of each individual, but the domi-

116   *Human Liberation in a Feminist Perspective*

nant thought pattern of modern society is the third stage.

In discussing models and typologies, we should remember that they are used in contemporary scientific theory as "a heuristic device to facilitate the productive organization and interpretation of experience."[37] Such typologies are conceptualizations. They do not so much directly represent the state of the world or particular human beings, as they are an imaginative construction by means of which the world can be better understood and organized. Thus the typologies under discussion are simply for the sake of analysis and do not represent rigid stages through which everyone must pass.

When Freire describes conscientization as beginning in the first awareness of human beings of the world around them, he calls this *doxa* (Greek for mere opinion, and belief).[38] In this stage people are still part of a mythical thought pattern and have not yet discovered the world as separate from themselves. Their historical consciousness is seen in that, although they are with and in the world, they still are aware of this reality and interested in looking at it and admiring it.

This naïve perception of reality then gives way to a critical awareness of the world which Freire calls *logos*. Here the subject begins to view the world as an object to be examined critically and to be analyzed in a new way. This corresponds to the ontological stage of historical consciousness in which human beings begin to look to forces beyond nature to provide meaning and power so that they can demythologize nature.

Thirdly, critical analysis leads to being in the world in order to transform it. This is the level of *praxis* which Freire describes as "a critical insertion into history" in order to transform the world. It is at the level of praxis that conscientization becomes a reality, for it is here that human beings begin to use their logos not only to understand and analyze but also to provide a means for action and change. Together with others they take on the role of subjects in a *functional* way so that they can "fashion their existence out of the material that life offers them."[39]

In order to keep this process of conscientization dynamic it is also necessary to make use of what Freire calls *utopia*. He does not speak of utopia in the Greek sense of "no place," but in the positive sense of a realistic vision of a "good place" or a future where there is "room to breathe" for those who are oppressed. Conscientization "turns the one conscientized into a utopian agent" who participates in "acts of denouncing and announcing—denouncing the dehumanizing structure and announcing the structure that will humanize."[40] It is this prophetic and helpful stance which keeps the future open for those who are engaged in a radical process of transforming the world.

Such hoping is only realistic when it is combined with praxis, but it forms an indispensable dynamic for continuing change in the face of the resistance of those whose interests are served by the status quo. It is dangerous, because utopian thinking can lead to new myths, and because it can also provide a dynamic that results in frustration, pain, and death in the face of the power of oppressive forces which seek to block the conscientization process toward liberation. Yet without it there can be no long-term commitment to continue the struggle against oppression, and the process of conscientization may become frozen into a new bureaucratic reform. In answer to the criticism of Thomas Sanders that liberation theology is "soft utopianism" and unrealistic in its goals, Rubem Alves supports the prophetic stance as a form of "realistic utopia" which refuses the fatalistic realism of accepting "facts" as they are.[41]

Dialectic of Liberation. In discussing the process of conscientization, Freire points to an important aspect of Marxian theory that should not be overlooked. It is not sufficient to change the social-economic-political *infrastructure* of society, because the old myths of the previous culture continue in people's minds as a *superstructure* which acts to defeat the changes.[42] This is why cultural revolution must include an ongoing process of conscientization that attacks the myths as well as the culture that has produced them. This process of changing people's minds as well as actions can be clearly seen in the description of consciousness-raising among women and blacks as a continuing *dialectic of liberation* in the self-awareness of individuals as well as groups.

In her article "Women's Liberation in Historical and Cultural Perspective" Rosemary Ruether describes this dialectic of liberation from the superstructures or mental structures of culture as a "struggle against cultural oppression."[43] Her description is similar to studies of acculturation by social anthropologists. She suggests that women and Third World groups go through a continuing dialectic with oppression in reaction against the projected images of the dominant society. The stages she lists in this dialectic are those of emulation, harking back to the past, and new communal personhood. In order to clarify more fully how self-awareness happens in relation to the cultural superstructures, it is important to look at the various stages in more detail, with particular emphasis on the feminist perspective.

Women and other groups often begin with an attitude toward the accepted roles of their culture which may be characterized as the *happy slave*. Here a woman sees herself as fulfilled in the accepted roles of mother, secretary, servant, sex symbol. In the face of suggestions about other options she is fearful and defensive and sees "women's lib" as a threat. Nelle Morton aptly describes this stage in the following way:

Women seem to go to great length to make clear to other women that even though life may be tough on them at times, in the long run all is well. They have been conditioned to be loyal at all costs to husband, children, boss, and colleagues. Irrelevant claims are exchanged: "I love my husband"; "I have been liberated for twenty-five years"; . . . "It is my choice to keep house"; . . . "Any woman can make it if she has what it takes."[44]

Or women and people of oppressed groups may perceive their cultural roles in such a way that they seek to gain equality with the "others" by *emulating the oppressor.* In this stage a person focuses attention away from her or his own group in order to devote all the energy possible to excellence of performance in order to "get ahead." Every group has such people who often have to be intelligent and hardworking, as well as lucky. For blacks these are the black colonialists, "Uncle Toms" or "oreo cookies" (black on the outside but white on the inside). Indian Americans call such people "apples"; Asians call them "bananas"; and so the list goes. Women in such a position are frequently referred to as "Aunt Thomasinas" or "marshmallow bunnies" (hard on the outside, but soft inside).[45] This type of "ideological scorn" is an indication that such a man or woman has surrendered to the status quo by accepting the old infrastructures and seeking to become like the respected white, Western male.

As women and Third World people discover that emulation, as a process of "liberation based on self-hatred," is "simply a capitulation to another side of enslavement," they react against the culture of oppression through forms of *rage.*[46] This rage stage which is an important aspect of self-liberation can be seen in Third World groups which sometimes destroy property and homes in a rejection of the alien culture. Out of such rage and frustration come ghetto riots, rebellions against "colonial acculturation," or forms of rebellion which Ruether describes as acting out "the underside of male dread."[47] Some women express their rage by joining groups such as SCUM, BITCH, or WITCH.[48] With most women, however, the rage is acted out in violent outbursts, anguished crying, or frightened withdrawal as they see the world into which they have been enculturated crumbling about them.[49]

Along with this rage, despair, and rejection of the oppressive superstructures comes a new search for *cultural identity* as groups begin to look to one another for support, and join together in a communal search for a usable future. As we have seen, this process of individual and group self-affirmation is an attempt to find a still living and evolving past which can help to shape the future in community with others. Third World groups return to their own national heritage to assert their sense of cultural worth and reject the oppressive standards of the outsider. Women not only seek identity in history but begin to seek out their sisters so that, in community, they can build a strong feminist culture which supports the ideas and actions of those who do not think persons are inferior because of their sex. Here the emphasis is on vertical support from the past and from women of the past, as well as horizontal support from sisters close by, and in every part of the globe. Efforts are made to integrate both mind and body in a new whole person who can act out a new way of life.[50]

The open-ended goal of the process of consciousness-raising is the discovery of *new awareness and ability to act* together with others to change both infrastructures and superstructures that deprive people of a usable future. As Ruether describes it:

In and through these various social interactions with oppression, however, I believe that all the rebellious groups in post-classical, post-Christian society are seeking a new communal personhood. . . .[51]

Because this is a human process of dialectic, it must include a continuing search for new possibilities of life in which the oppressor and oppressed are included. This means the development of new forms of dialogue and community as well as new consciousness. Peggy Way describes this continuing search in her own ministry by saying, that the

. . . authority of my ministry is in my rooted participation as a free and emerging person engaged in examining the processes of human existence, testing out their principles and traditions, and experiencing the possibilities of new creations of persons, institutions and cultures.[52]

As we conclude this description of the search for liberation and blessing in the contemporary lives of oppressed people, it is important to emphasize that neither the dialectic of liberation nor the process of conscientization is simply linear. It continues in a variety of forms and rarely proceeds exactly in the stages indicated by heuristic typologies. Often those who find that the odds against them are too great return to former stages of quietism. Sometimes new awareness comes to people at a stage in their lives or culture in which the rage and rejection stage may be less violent because they have already moved toward self-acceptance of their full personhood. Rarely is this a purely individual process, for human beings depend on others to help shape their attitudes and actions, and ultimately Christians trust in a God who cares enough about them to give them a future and a hope.

CONVERSION AND EVANGELISM

The search for liberation and blessing moves toward the goal of full human personhood in community with others (*shalom*). It takes place both at the level of the human traditioning process and at the level of God's traditioning of Jesus Christ as the Liberator. In both cases women and men discover signs of *shalom*, or wholeness, in their lives through a process of self-transcendence and opening themselves up to a new reality. It remains for us then to look at the relation of the two traditioning processes: first, to examine the way in which God hands over Jesus Christ into the hands of all generations and nations by comparing the ways that *conscientization and conversion* happen in human experience; second, to examine the way that liberation theology can help us to participate in God's traditioning by comparing *praxis and evangelism*.

Conscientization and Conversion. In the analysis of conscientization as a process of coming to new consciousness and new ability to take action to transform our lives and world, it is readily apparent that this is parallel to the Christian experience of conversion. Thus Philip Potter says that in the process of cultural revolution

... the language of salvation has been used, as observers point out. In Latin America, this process has taken the form of *conscientization,* the means by which people become conscious of themselves as human beings capable of shaping their destiny and of doing so for the common good.[53]

The Old Testament describes the experience of conversion *(shub)* as returning to the original covenant relation of Yahweh and the people of God. For the prophets, conversion or repentance was a total reorientation of the entire person and a return to Yahweh which led to obedience and unqualified trust in God.[54] Thus Jer. 8:4 reads: "When ... [people] fall, do they not rise again? If one turns away, does he [or she] not return?" And Ezek. 33:19 says, "And when the wicked turns from ... wickedness, and does what is lawful and right he [or she] shall live by it."

The New Testament translation of the Hebrew words for repentance is frequently *metanoia,* or changed mind. Other words used of repentance carry the similar meaning of turning around or conversion. The difference in the New Testament is not in the process itself, but in the fact that the demand for repentance is set in the context of a new possibility for a life of obedience under the rulership of God that is being initiated by Jesus. In Mark 1:15, Jesus announces that the time has come. "The time is fulfilled, and the kingdom of God is at hand; repent, and believe in the gospel." Conversion is turning away *(epistrophē)* from all powers that claim allegiance, to an obedience of faith in the one and only living God whose rulership one accepts *(metanoia,* Rom. 1:5). It is a process of coming to complete trust in the love of God in

Jesus Christ or to faith. Faith is at once a gift of God's grace, and also a complete personal response to this offer of salvation and liberation.

In Biblical and ecclesial tradition, stories of dramatic conversions leading not only to new names but also to new lifestyles are abundant. They show the experience of the liberating power of God which breaks open the lives of men and women, bringing new health, wholeness, joy, and deliverance so that people truly begin even now to live in a new age. The same experience of new life and liberating power is seen in the process of conscientization. Harvey Cox writes:

Millions of poor people are beginning to see themselves for the first time as the active subject of history rather than as its passive recipients. This new way of seeing the self and the world is an example of what we in theology call "metanoia" or conversion.[55]

In conscientization there is also a radical reorientation, a turning around in a process filled with emotions of both fear and joy. Morton recalls the words used by women to describe the coming to consciousness:

In reflecting on the experience thus far one is struck with expressions as "a dam breaking," "erupting of a volcano," "a burst from inside," accompanied by gestures which may be characterized as spontaneous—far from calculated risk.[56]

Here too in conscientization there is a whole new understanding of the meaning of life which leads to rebirth as a new person.

In conscientization we find the traditional theological description of the *ordo salutis* played out in a new form. There is the experience of *justification* or being accepted through grace. There is also the continuing struggle for *regeneration* and *sanctification* through obedient action.[57] As one woman explained in a paraphrase from Freire: "Each of us has to give her witness, and conscientization is a summons to do that: to be new each day. Hence it is *peace,* and it enables us to understand others."

There is no doubt that a formal analogy exists between conversion and conscientization in the way they happen in human experience. The difference is one of emphasis. In conversion stress is placed on God's action while in conscientization stress is placed on human initiative. Although the subject of conversion is the Tradition of God, and the subject of conscientization is the tradition of a new communal consciousness and power for change, the process is similar and the Holy Spirit can and does work through both. Such a comparison is made by Carol Christ and Marilyn Collins:

Conversion to women's liberation is structurally similar to conversion to a new religious consciousness. In this sense, women's liberation itself partakes of the numinous. Like other conversion experiences it is frightening as well as liberating. Social structures and institutions which had defined social reality are experienced as arbitrary and alienating. The center of reality changes.[58]

It is interesting to note the analogy between coming to consciousness and coming to faith or trust in God through Jesus Christ. In classical reformation theology faith was spelled out under three interrelated rubrics.[59] These include: *notitia* as taking notice of the actions of God in Jesus Christ, or knowledge of this Tradition; *assensus* as consent or commitment to this Tradition by active participation; *fiducia* as complete trust or confidence in this Tradition. The three words and their different emphases are all dimensions of the New Testament word *pistis* ("faith"). Together they form the happening of faith which is the gift of God.

These same elements are clear in Freire's typology of the process of conscientization: *logos,* or critical awareness, corresponds to *notitia; praxis,* or commitment to action-reflection, is similar to *assensus;* and *utopia,* or the vision of trust which makes possible a transformed self and world, corresponds to *fiducia*. Together they make up the same important whole in the process of new life.

God hands over Jesus Christ through the power of the Holy Spirit, and this handing over finds its response in conversion and transformed lives. This same process can go on in human relationships which bring about new life that is shared with others in a common action of human traditioning that in itself may be a sign of *shalom*, pointing back to God's liberating concern.

Praxis and Evangelism. The Mission of God in handing over Jesus Christ demonstrates God's shalomatic purpose to bring liberation and blessing to all humanity. In Christ the redemption of the world has been accomplished and the decisive victory won. Yet in a world still groaning, that redemption has to be accepted as liberation and blessing and lived out as *shalom* by those who hear the Word of God's love and accept it in faith. The Mission continues in the midst of history by the power of the Holy Spirit, and the community of faith seeks to participate in this traditioning action of God by pointing to where God seems to be "happening" in the world.

This participation in God's Mission by the church is usually called *evangelism:* sharing the good news of God's liberation in Jesus Christ. It is this task of evangelism which is the focus of liberation theologies as their *praxis* methodology leads them to *do and tell liberation*.[60]

Action coupled with reflection is not a program to be accomplished and forgotten. It is an evangelical attitude toward life itself; an attitude that looks at what is going on in situations of oppression, trying constantly to see the problems and to work out the way in which God's will of liberation can be done; only to begin again with the next set of problems and consequent actions.

Over the last few decades some people have become used to speaking of the "four-fold witness of evangelism" as:

kērygma, diakonia, koinōnia, and *leitourgia.*[61] These forms of witness to the Messianic Mission of God illustrate the ever-changing and overlapping dimensions of communicating the gospel. Through *kērygma* the Word is proclaimed so that the story of Jesus of Nazareth is told in relation to the particular situation in which people find themselves. In this way people are challenged to accept the life-style of Jesus and be liberated for *diakonia* or service to others. *Shalom* is made present and proclaimed in the story of the Prince of Shalom by those who let their actions become demonstrations of liberation and hope on behalf of others. In describing *diakonia,* Hans Hoekendijk writes:

The whole story of the New Testament revolves around this one theme. Now, at last, someone has come *not* to be served. That would be an old story; that we know. But *He came to serve.* Everything that was done by this Son of Man (Mark 10:45) who came to serve, including humiliation, self-empty-ing, *cross,* death is summarized in one final communique of eight letters: *diakonia.*[62]

Through *koinōnia* the wholeness of life in community with Christ and others is lived out, not in any one single pattern, but in ways that create signs of *shalom* and meaningful community in a world full of division. For instance, the "snapshot pictures" Luke gives us in Acts 2:42–47; 4:32–37 describe the life-style of the early Christian church in their particular setting. Luke intends to show by these pictures that through the power of Christ's Spirit the Christian *koinōnia* fulfills all the ideals of the Greek and Israelite community life. This life is the basis of their participation in mission as they move out to the "end of the earth" (Acts 1:8). Through *leitourgia* the witness of *kērygma, diakonia,* and *koinōnia* is celebrated with joy and thanksgiving, and *shalom* is both lived and shared with others.

These overlapping dimensions for communicating the gospel are very much a part of God's liberating action. They point to ways of participation in that Mission. "In kerygma, koinonia and diakonia," according to Moltmann, "the Spirit of freedom and of the coming kingdom is brought into all the misery of today."[63]

The word "evangelism" has many meanings in the minds of those who use it, besides that of the root meaning of *euangelion* (communicating the good news). Fackre points out that the various fruits of evangelism are often mistaken for its roots:

> Thus, some, recognizing that the Evangel transforms lives, treat its communication first and foremost as a program for "converting sinners," with the use of manipulative methods that regularly degenerate into sales campaigns and scalp collecting. Some recognizing that evangelism does make for growth in the Body of Christ, interpret it, first and foremost as recruitment of new members for the institutional church. Others, seeing that the gospel does turn people toward Jericho roads, translate it without remainder into social action or social service. And yet others, who know the story breeds new joy and high feeling, reduce evangelism to the cultivation of inner experiences and testimony thereto. . . . Each of these puts the cart before the horse. . . . Evangelism is, first and foremost, the scatter-act. It is getting the news out. . . .[64]

One of the ways of seeking to prevent the various dimensions of evangelism from becoming one-sided in the life of the church is to remember that the work of evangelism is derived, not primarily from our own actions alone, but from God's traditioning action whose goal is *shalom* for all humanity. Evangelism flows out of *theocentric* participation in God's love affair with the world. It is not first of all *ecclesiocentric*. The church's role is to point to Christ in the world and not to itself.[65] Another way to prevent reductionism of various kinds is to continue to focus on the meaning of evangelism as the totality of God's concern for liberation and blessing in all aspects of human life, both social and individual, both physical and spiritual. A third way to retain the fullness of the communication of the gospel is to remember that the gospel is *contextual* or situation-variable. In each situation the meaning of the good news speaks concretely, about particular needs for liberation and speaks in the language, life-style, and social structures of that particular place (I Cor. 9:19–21). Shoki Coe writes:

Contextuality, therefore, I believe, is that critical assessment of what makes the context really significant in the light of the *Missio Dei*. It is the missiological discernment of the signs of the times, seeing where God is at work and calling us to participate in it.[66]

Liberation theology can be helpful in maintaining the full dimensions of evangelism. This theology begins from a theocentric basis as reflection on the liberating action of God, and seeks by means of praxis to focus on social as well as individual needs of persons and groups. Above all, liberation theologians are committed to share in the situations of oppression in order to make both hoping and planning a means of bringing new life and freedom.[67] Ahron Sapezian points to this when he says, "If rootedness is the starting point, *commitment* to the dispossessed in their struggle for emancipation is the basic *ethical stance* in the 'theology of liberation.' "[68] For liberation theology the key issue is not *orthodoxy* but *"orthopraxy."* Without denying the importance of disciplined, logical, and documented reflection on the meaning of Biblical and ecclesial tradition, it is basically concerned, not with reformulation of doctrines, but with the challenge of giving form to the message of good news as a praxis of liberation on behalf of others. As Freire has pointed out, praxis is dialectical. Action without reflection degenerates into unthinking activism, and reflection without action degenerates into verbalism.[69] Nevertheless the locus of the praxis is to be found in the situation of oppression. As Sapezian puts it:

. . . theology has to do more with obeying the Gospel than with defining, prescribing, or defending it; orthodoxy cannot be a substitute for orthopraxis; sharing in the effective transformation of life and of institutions and structures that shape life cannot be endlessly postponed by intellectual gamesmanship.[70]

The dangers of one-sided evangelism are also present, however, in liberation theologies, and even more so, because they make use of ideologies that are important in the process of social change. Just as evangelism can degenerate into narrow proselytism which sees its purpose solely as recruitment of members, liberation theologies, and movements of which they are a part, often become focused only on the mobilization of people for a particular cause. They tend to forget that ultimately the cause is transcended by God's cause of eschatological mission.[71] In the same way the practice of evangelism sometimes becomes a form of propaganda designed to "create people in our own image" instead of letting the love of God become incarnated into peoples' own life-styles and culture.[72] Liberation theologies have this same tendency when their social concern degenerates only into a form of ideology which all people are supposed to accept.

It helps us to avoid these dangers when we remember that traditioning itself has a double meaning. The handing over *(paradidonai)* of Christ can mean *betrayal* to the cross as well as sharing God's victorious love with others.[73] Participation in God's traditioning calls for constant care not to betray that Tradition by false methods of handing over, or evangelism which become barriers to the hearing and living out of the good news of liberation.

There is no *one* foolproof method of living out the Truth. But at least liberation theology expresses the heart of the traditioning process as *hope-in-action*.[74] In this view the task of evangelism is to participate in the Messianic work of Jesus Christ so that hope in the future which God holds open for us is translated into actions on behalf of the defuturized of society. In this way liberation theology can help to raise up signs in the world of God's plans of liberation and blessing for humanity. For, as Jeremiah has reminded us, God does have plans, plans "for *(shalom)* and not for evil, to give you a future and a hope" (Jer. 29:11).

5: INCARNATION
AND HUMANIZATION

The "ferment of freedom" which is experienced in the restlessness and alienation of people in every part of the world is an expression of the search for the meaning of life. No longer is that meaning to be taken for granted. In a historicized world men and women have to shape their own understanding of what it is to be human out of their actions and visions of a humane society. Most Christians and non-Christians live in a world where there is no one vision of humankind; a world where visions have to be worked out in the midst of life.

Looking at thought patterns of the past and the present we can see how people have experienced, not only reality but also their own humanity in different forms. In the mythical thought world existence was understood as unified with the powers of the universe. People saw their humanity as a dependence on nature, of which they were a part. In the metaphysical stage the search for meaningful existence was focused on the place of persons in the separated worlds of nature and supernature. In the functional style of secular society this search goes on as men and women develop partnerships in shaping the events of the world with which they interact.

If we look around us in the world today, we see not only this variety, culminating in the restlessness of the functional or historical stage of existence, but also the variety of political, cultural, and national ideologies that are used to describe reality in such a way that people become what is described. A similar kind of ideological search is evident in the women's liberation movement as women begin to explain the meaning of existence in reference to the experience of sisterhood.[1]

Even those who look to the Bible for the clarification of humanization discover a series of images and stories that point to an ever-growing and changing understanding of personhood in relation to God. "In the last analysis," according to Juan Luis Segundo, people as they appear in the course of history are "borne along by the love of God." This does not define human existence but "enlightens us on the meaning of our existence."[2] In this perspective God's will to be with us as *Emmanuel* presents the opportunity and possibility of a search for new humanity in the changing world in which we live.

In spite of obvious indications from many societies and nations that there can be no one description of humanization, we have seen that there are at least three ingredients which seem important to this process. People need some possibility of participation in understanding and shaping the world in which they live and the future of that world. They need support communities which help them to grow and to find out who they are. They also need to be accepted by others and themselves as subjects and persons, and not simply as objects of manipulation or functions of society. These three ingredients of human wholeness can aid us in reflecting on the *search for true humanity* in the light of participation in shaping the future. They also point us to the emergence of community as illustrated in the struggle of women toward *sisterhood on the way to servanthood* and to the meaning of *partnership and humanization* as the experience of becoming subjects and whole persons.

SEARCH FOR TRUE HUMANITY

The search for true humanity takes place in all aspects of life: past, present, and future. Yet this search is basically future-oriented. The *truly human* is also the *newly human;* the vision of new righteousness, peace, and justice in community. For liberation theology this vision is shaped by a "memory of the future" which provides a glimpse of new personhood. This memory begins with the Old Testament understanding of *shalom* as the *restoration of created humanity.* It continues in the story of the One who came as a *representative of the new humanity* who points us toward the goal of God's liberating action. And it frees us to participate in becoming, ourselves, representatives of that new life in which there will be neither oppressor nor oppressed, but only man and woman in the process of liberation.

Restoration of Created Humanity. In the Old Testament the understanding of what it means to be a person is linked to the knowledge of the *humanity of God.* This humanity, according to Karl Barth, is the expression of God's relation to, and turning toward, human beings.[3] It was experienced in the context of Yahweh's actions in history and dialogue with the Hebrew people. The living God was known through the *togetherness of God with humankind.* This togetherness is an indication of a will to liberate and bless the people in fulfillment of God's shalomatic purpose among the nations. John I. Durham expresses this when he says:

Shalom refers to . . . [one's] realization, under the blessing of God, of the plan with which God has endowed . . . [one] and the potential with which God has endowed . . . [one]. As such, it would be the perfection towards which God has directed . . . [humanity] and to which . . . [God] alone can draw . . . [them]. . . . Shalom is the faithful human reaction to the presence of God; the beginning and sequence and end of "humanization."[4]

In order to restore the blessing of Adam and Eve and their responsible partnership in caring for creation, God intervenes on the scene of disobedience and dehumanization by choosing Abraham to become the one through whom the blessing will be mediated (Gen. 1:27–28; 12:1–2; 9:8–17). Without attempting to distinguish between the various traditions of blessing, or elaborate on the understanding of covenant as a suzerainty treaty in the Ancient Near East, it is possible to point to the understanding of the writers of the Old Testament that Abraham and his descendants became covenant partners with God, with the task of giving human meaning to the world. The vision of this task was often obscured in Israel's history; the prophetic witness served to remind the people of their role in God's concern for all the nations and Israel's task as a source of blessing within the *oikoumenē* (world, Amos 9:7; Isa. 19:25; 42:6).[5]

The Biblical word "nations" does not refer to national governments as we know them today, but to every human grouping on the face of the earth. God's will is to be together with people wherever they gather, in whatever institution, to realize the humanity of God in a togetherness that restores the relationship of created personhood. This same will to be with us is seen in God's continued traditioning action in handing over Jesus Christ to all generations and all groupings. In the Bible the nations are always on the scene as witnesses to what happens between God and Israel, and in the eschatological proclamation they will all be ultimately included in God's humanizing activity. To be a person is understood as being invited into the procession of all human groupings; to be "judged" and to "walk in Yahweh's path" (Isa. 2:1–4). The idea of the nations' pilgrimage to Zion is fairly constant in the Old Testament tradition (Micah 4:1–3; Isa. 49:6).[6]

Through the history of God's dealings with Israel and the "nations," we can catch a glimpse of the Hebrew as *Everyone*. This is possible, according to Porteous, because

... the Hebrew in the circle of the chosen people of God found himself [and herself] confronted and challenged by God, and in this relationship learned what it is essential that ... [persons] should know about ... [themselves]; and what God ultimately demands of all ... [people].[7]

The restoration of personhood was experienced again and again in Israel's life as God established and renewed the covenant and fulfilled the promise of deliverance and blessing in the history of the exodus, the Babylonian exile and return, and beyond. In spite of unfaithfulness and suffering the experience of the Hebrew people was always a cause of new hope in God. Each promise, as it was fulfilled, brought with it an *overspill* of new promise or memory of the future.[8] Thus the promise of the restoration of creation moved ahead of Israel like a horizon of hope, pointing not only back to restoration but also forward to a time when God would create "new heavens and a new earth" (Isa. 65:17).

Representation of New Humanity. In liberation theology the search for true personhood finds its most important clues in the memory of the future reflected in the New Testament witness to Jesus Christ as the representative of new humanity and Prince of Shalom (Eph. 2:14–18; Isa. 9:6; Luke 2:11; John 14:27). The affirmation of the New Testament writers is that, in Christ, God has decisively entered history and changed that history (Col. 1:19). God's fulfillment of the promise to redeem all creation has happened representatively in Jesus Christ, even though the promise looks forward again to the completion of that work and calls all people to faithful participation in the ongoing event of humanization.[9]

The humanity of God seen through Yahweh's *self-presentation* to Moses and the Hebrew people in Exodus is now actualized in the *re-presentation* in Immanuel (Isa. 7:14; Matt. 1:23). God's intention to be together with all people is lived out in word and deed in the story of Jesus Christ so that all people can come to know the truth about themselves and God's intended future (I Tim. 2:4; Rom. 8:31–39). The Gospel accounts of Jesus have woven record and confession into one, according to Günther Bornkamm.

By this they show that they took Jesus himself, in all his words and even apart from them, as *the* Word of God in the world (Jn. 1:1; I Jn. 1:1); Jesus himself, prior to and in all his works *the* work of God in the world; Jesus himself, prior to and in all the stories the decisive and final history of God in the world.[10]

Through God's will to be together with people, Jesus Christ becomes *God's re-presentation* of the humanity of God. Just because of this he is also God's chosen *representative of true humanity* as togetherness with God. As Dorothee Sölle points out in her book *Christ the Representative*, this work of Christ has been dealt with in theological tradition under the "rubric of Christ's mediatorial office." "Representatively he reconciled us to God and revealed God's prevenient grace toward us."[11] This concept can be seen in the whole course of God's dealings with people: first, through Israel or the remnant as the representative of the many by the minority; ultimately, in the representation of the many by the One.[12] But the re-presentation of God to us and of us to God has an additional overspill in ongoing history. God also continues to look to us to *become re-presentatives* of true humanity. Our dependence on representation issues in responsibility for representation. As Sölle puts it, Jesus Christ "is a representative not a replacement."[13] God's choice of the *One* also opens up a new possibility of a future in which *all* can become representative of a new personhood.

In the life, death, and resurrection of Jesus of Nazareth the whole of our predicament is focused so that we have not only a perspective on life in all its humanizing and dehumanizing aspects but also a possibility of hope against hope. The Gospel stories of healing and forgiveness such as that of the paralytic or the Gerasene demoniac are indicators of the possibility of a new life and history which has its beginning in healing and faith (Matt. 9:2–8; Mark 5:1–20). In Christ, God has chosen for our future, not only forgiving sins, but also helping us to choose for new life. Jesus' representation of "old humanity" before God and "new humanity" before us was not easy for him, nor is our task of representation easy. This representation includes suffering and the cross as the central element. Käsemann reminds us that it is under the cross that we come to ourselves, because that is the place where God is revealed as Creator.[14] This cross is the central *skandalon* of the gospel, for it shows the cost of God's humanity in suffering with us and for us and challenges us to identification with, and representation of, one who suffers for others (I Cor. 1:18–25).

The central scandal of the cross raises the question of the *scandal of particularity* which is characteristic of all God's actions in and through history. In God's togetherness with us, particular people and events become the bearers of meaning, not only because of, but in spite of, their concrete particularity in the history of one small group of people, or one wandering Jewish rabbi. In speaking of John's use of the symbol of *logos* to express the meaning of Jesus as the manifestation of ultimate reality, E. C. Blackman writes:

The eternal thus entering history, and being, as it were, concentrated in a single human life, poses an insuperable philosophical problem, admittedly. This aspect of the Incarnation has been called, in G. Kittel's memorable phrase, the "scandal of particularity."[15]

For women the scandal is seen not just in Jesus' Jewishness or his obscurity in the world of the first century, but most importantly in his *maleness*.[16] Jesus was born as a male *(anēr)*. How is it possible for this male to be the bearer of God's togetherness with women and men when he represents only one half of the human race in this respect? One possibility in approaching this question is to get rid of the scandal by looking for a further incarnation in the form of a woman.[17] Another is to say that Jesus was just a "good person" and not uniquely the "representative of new humanity." As such his particularity is of no great importance to the question of salvation, and women are free to look farther for more meaningful, feminine role models such as those of the Mother Goddess in ancient religions.

For women who affirm with many other liberation theologies that Christ is the subject of Christian theology and the unique representative of God's humanity, the scandal remains in all its particularity! According to Norman Perrin: "The Christian faith as such is committed to the paradoxical assertion that a historical event within time, Jesus and his cross, is the eschatological event."[18] If women make their stand with Christ, the Representative, they must struggle to make clear that Christ's work was not first of all that of being a male but that of being the new human. It is also important to recognize that in an androcentric culture and a patriarchal religion, God, perhaps, chose to send the representative as a male in order for him to have the freedom to live and work as a rabbi.

Beyond this, Christian women can see in Jesus a unique revelation of true personhood: One who helped both men and women to understand their own total personhood.[19] The life of Jesus displays characteristics of love, compassion, and caring often considered to be cultural characteristics of women. In his own life he was a "feminist" in the sense that he considered men and women equal; equal in their need to be helped, and equal in their need to be pointed toward the new future of God's Kingdom (Luke 10:38–42; John 4:7–30).[20] This is not beside the point, because it demonstrates Jesus' ability to be a whole person who brought that possibility to others.[21] To think of Christ first in terms of his male sex or his racial origin is to revert again to a *biological determinism* which affirms that the most important thing about a person is her or his sex or color. The most important affirmation of ourselves and of Jesus is that we want to be accepted as subjects and persons, within whom biological differentiation is a secondary aspect.

Paul's understanding of Jesus Christ as the New Adam *(anthrōpos)* is important for the interpretation of his work as representative. Paul uses a variety of metaphors to express the meaning of the incarnation which point to the understanding "that he is God's representative, through whom the divine plan for human redemption is made operative."[22] In Rom. 5:12–21 and I Cor. 15:45–49 Christ is seen as realizing the ideal of the First Human as he opens up new possibilities for human life.

> The first human is from the earth, a human of dust; the second human is from heaven. . . . As was the human of dust, so are those who are of the dust; and as is the human from heaven, so are those who are of heaven. Just as we have borne the image of the human of dust, we shall also bear the image of the human of heaven.[23]

Christ's achievement of new humanity through the incarnation and the resurrection is available to those who participate with him through faith. The image of representative becomes an invitation to come of age and take responsibility for our representative role by working to help bring liberation and blessing into the lives of all people including ourselves. We join in God's work of liberation by reflecting on the meaning of that liberation in the lives of those who find themselves dehumanized.[24] In this way the representatives of true humanity become women and men who take responsibility for joining Christ and others as signs of the power and possibility of participation in shaping the future.

> I have been crucified with Christ; it is no longer I who live, but Christ who lives in me; and the life I now live in the flesh

I live by faith in the Son of God, who loved me and gave himself for me. (Gal. 2:20.)

SISTERHOOD ON THE WAY TO SERVANTHOOD

Servanthood presents problems for women and other oppressed groups who have been condemned to play a servant role not of their own choosing. For these groups humanization is experienced, not so much through service, as through bonding together in supportive communities that can provide new identity and hope. Among women it is the process of coming to *sisterhood* by learning to affirm oneself and one's sister in her aspirations, whatever the divergence of race, language, geography, ideology, and tactics, which provides a key to humanization.[25]

Servanthood, Not Subordination. The role of servant in both the Old and New Testaments is not an indication of inferiority or subordination. *Diakonia* is the acceptance of someone else's life project as your own scenario or story. A helper (*'ezer*) or servant (*'ebed*) is frequently the one who is an instrument of divine help to someone else's need.[26] Similar significance is attached to the idea of Israel as a chosen people. "For you are a people holy to the LORD your God; the LORD your God has chosen you to be a people for . . . [God's] own possession, out of all the peoples that are on the face of the earth." (Deut. 7:6.) The privilege of God's gracious choice is a privilege of *election for service*. Israel is to be an instrument for making God's love known to all the nations.

This form of God's blessing becomes very clear in *'ebed Yahweh* hymns. "Behold my servant, whom I uphold, my chosen, in whom my soul delights; I have put my Spirit upon him, he will bring forth justice to the nations." (Isa. 42:1.) In ancient Near Eastern texts the word *'ebed* connotes a certain honor and distinction, so that one may boast of this title especially if one is a servant of a highly placed person such as a king or a god. The word is used of all kinds of persons who stand in a particular relation to Yahweh in the Old Testament, and suggests that the bearer of the title has a particular charge from God. In *'ebed Yahweh* hymns the word not only indicates a charge or task but also implies that group or person is chosen or elected.[27] This servant of Yahweh is chosen to be a suffering servant in order to bear "the sin of many" (Isa. 53:12).

Regardless of whether the Suffering Servant is to be identified with Israel or a remnant or one person or all of them, in the Gospels we find an identification of this role with Jesus. Although he might not have called himself the *'ebed Yahweh,* Jesus appears to have a growing consciousness of the necessity of his own vicarious death as reflected in the Gospel passages about the suffering of the Son of Man (Matt. 12:15–21; 17:9–13).[28] Perhaps Paul is also echoing this view of Christ in Phil. 2:7 when he exhorts the congregation to humility and service by speaking of the example of Christ as one who "emptied himself, taking the form of a servant (*doulos,* slave)." This service to others on behalf of God was not a form of subordination to other people, but rather a free offering of self and acceptance of service and love in return (Luke 7:36–50; 8:1–3; 10:38–42).[29]

The word "apostle" in Pauline texts carries the same implication of one who has been chosen to serve as a witness of the gospel. For this reason Paul speaks of Phoebe, Apollos, and himself as *diakonoi,* or representatives of Christ the servant (Rom. 1:1; 16:1–2; I Cor. 3:5). In fact he even calls himself a slave *(doulos)* of Christ because this indicates his role as a participant in God's liberating action with Christ (I Cor. 9:19; II Cor. 4:5). In the New Testament and in church history women have been referred to, not only as servants but also as *apostles* (witnesses) of Christ. For instance, in Rom. 16:7, Junias is considered by many scholars to have been a woman. The first witnesses of the resurrection who ran to tell the good news were women (Luke 24:1–10). Some of the church fathers speak of these women as well as the Samaritan woman as apostles (John 4:28–29). Mary Magdalene was even called "the apostle to the apostles."[30]

Regardless of what the role of servant has come to mean in the history of church and society, in the Bible it is clearly a role of honor and responsibility to take part in God's work of service in the world. Women and men are called by God in Jesus Christ to be both servants and apostles as representatives of the new humanity. In this view the real scandal of being a servant or representative is not that of subordination but of *suffering*. The cost of representation in the midst of oppression is the suffering of God and of men and women for others.

Sisterhood and Servanthood. *Diakonia* is not only a part of the gospel story of liberation, it is also an indication of what it means to become more fully human in freedom for others. According to the example of Jesus, to be truly human is to live in love and service toward others and toward God. Yet the clarity of this idea in Scripture does not easily dispel the problems which the idea of servanthood presents for women and other oppressed groups as they struggle against roles of subordination in church and society.

Women and others in modern society do not like the idea of servanthood because they see it as an expression of their own *powerlessness*. Too long they have actually been servants of *men*. Social structures have dictated the subordinate roles which women were allowed to play, and the church male hierarchies have claimed divine sanction for these roles. Even the word "service" itself has become so debased in its common usage today that men and women alike often think of it only as referring to a "Band-Aid" type assistance. They have begun to speak of "social action" and "change agents" to describe a concern for others which expresses itself in attempts to change the power structures that oppress and deprive people of their rights.

The predominantly white male clergy have used their position of power to reinforce an inferior servant role on all the laity, as well as religious orders. Although the *laos* in the original sense includes *all* the people of God without distinction between ordained and unordained, the present structures of church life place the unordained (of which the majority are women) in the position of providing support services for the clergy.[31] No matter how significant a women's organization or religious order may become because of its service or dedication, it remains subject to the structural or canonical limitations of churches which are ultimately controlled by men.

This situation frequently hampers the type and quality of service which women are able to render in the mission of the church. One of the ways to begin to change this, however, is to refuse to accept this situation of powerlessness and to reclaim the true meaning of service as the basis for partnership in the church. It is important to be clear that *diakonia* is in fact the basis of genuine ecclesial power and authority. This is why Pope Gregory I called himself "the servant of the servants of God." The only genuine form of power in the church is that of service. It is the power of inner authority which comes to those who are willing to "put their bodies on the line" ("present your bodies as a living sacrifice," Rom. 12:1).

The opposite of service, according to Hans Küng, is domination and misuse of power.[32] Or to turn it around, the opposite of domination is service or liberation! Women's liberation is not seeking domination and misuse of power, because women know that they will not have moved society toward new humanity and liberation if they have simply replaced one oppressor with another.

The process of overcoming false domination in the name of genuine service or liberation is a difficult one for women. It can, however, be a process of coming to *sisterhood on the way to servanthood.* It begins with the women who become aware of the false contradictions in their situation and risk taking action. In coming to new awareness women must first learn to reject the role of submission to men and to affirm their own full humanity. Mary Daly says, "What we are about is the human becoming of that half of the human race that has been excluded from humanity by sexual definition."[33] Submission is in fact an element of sinfulness in which women refuse to accept their full created status as partners with men in the work of God's mission in the world. The assumption that service equals subordination is a form of "naïve consciousness" and must be replaced by "sororal community-consciousness."[34] Interpretations such as that of Karl Barth that assert that man and woman were created as co-human, yet that woman is always second in God's order of creation have to be challenged if we are to assert our full co-humanity.[35] Women have to be clear with themselves and their sisters around the world about the distinction between God's ordering of creation and cultural expressions of various societies.

They are challenged to accept sisterhood as applying to themselves and other women, so they can begin to have a genuine approach to service as reflecting the role of "divine helper." Once they learn to accept their own identity as women, and to work out their own life-styles in community with other women, then they are also able to find new ways of cooperating with men in being *God's* servants on behalf of all humanity. In this way women begin to liberate themselves together with others in order to become free for others.

Ultimately this can lead us to be not only *pro-woman* but also *pro-human,* and to accept a genuine reciprocal relationship of service. Such a relationship would be modeled on the life-style of Jesus of Nazareth so that women are set free both to serve and to be served without loss of identity or fear of subordination. Through shared learning that sisterhood is both beautiful and powerful, women can join men as partners in recognizing that servanthood is beautiful and powerful for those who accept both its risk and cost!

PARTNERSHIP AND HUMANIZATION

Being accepted as a subject is another part of the process of humanization. Human meaning is derived from interaction between subjects and the world. People are not just *in* the world, they stand out from the world in order to interact *with* it, especially in a functional or historicized existence. The responsibility of caring for the world, naming it and giving it meaning, can be distorted as men and women make irresponsible choices about their environment and people in their struggle for survival. This seems to be indicated in the etiological myth of the Fall in which the harmonious relation of man and woman and all creation is ruptured (Gen., chs. 1 to 3). "Peace in existence" is transformed into a "struggle for existence" in the face of death and finitude.[36] This struggle includes the dislocation of the relationship between man and woman and the earth.

The domination-subjugation relationship is an indicator of this polarization and struggle. It transforms the oppressed group into the *Others* who cease to be accepted as subjects in their own right and become objects of manipulation. In an androcentric culture, as Simone de Beauvoir points out, the *Other* becomes the woman who stands as a threat to the dominant male, even as she is desired and needed by him.[37] In a technological society dominated by white Western cultures, Third World peoples also become the *Other*. Their lives, lands, and future are to be controlled and exploited by those who have the power to use them. Harvey Cox says:

Man's domination of women is the oldest and most persistent and maybe the most basic form of seignioralty. It suffuses all societies with the bacillus of over-under hegemony and

therefore fuels both racial tyrannies and the corporate cali-
phates that despoil the people of the Third World.[38]

In discussing the question of partnership and humanization, we must keep in mind that only as people are accepted
and accept themselves as subjects and not objects is there a
possibility of true partnership. Only as we work together in
community to find such partnership in liberation can we
grow into co-humanity. The basic polarity of *authority-sub-
mission* has to be challenged at its root: the dislocation of
human beings in their relation to one another. In this way
new patterns of relationship can be constructed. This is the
radical goal of liberation theology and of feminist theology as
LaVonne Althouse has indicated.

Feminism asks us to look at role-definition and the authority-
submission design for human relationships and raise questions about them. It affirms that this design and role-definition do not really support, improve, protect or uphold social
institutions. Rather, feminists say, some miracle preserves
society and its institutions in spite of rigid insistence on en-
forcing these roles and this design which distort both men's
and women's personalities.[39]

From a feminist point of view of equality between the
sexes, it is necessary for us first to examine the problems
raised in the objectification of sex roles through cultural definitions of *feminine* which are projected on the *female* members of the human race. Then we can take a new look at the
possibility of both men and women finding their way toward
partnership and humanization so that they become *not lonesome, but twosome.* In our exploration it is important to bear
in mind that the male-female relationships under discussion
have analogies to other oppressor-oppressed relationships.
The man-woman dislocation is symptomatic of many situations in which the oppressed are seen, and see themselves,
as the *Other.*

Female and Feminine. In discussing the problem of sex-role objectification, we should bear in mind the distinction between female and feminine. *Female* refers to the biological characteristics of women. *Feminine* refers to a variety of psychological and cultural characteristics which are associated with the woman in a particular society. There is no clear agreement about what constitutes basic psychological or cultural characteristics of women because these are always studied within the context of an enculturation process which has affected the way a particular woman expresses her feminine characteristics.

It is well known that a culture selects from only a small segment of the wide possibilities in its elaboration of the sex roles and the divisions of labor.[40] Sometimes in certain tribal culture we find that the roles and personality traits that are considered "normal" in Western society are reversed.[41] The investigation of ancient myths and rituals in which women play a leading role as the ones who are the preservers of life also point to a matriarchal way of life. But there is no clear evidence that ancient myths can be directly translated into ancient sociology or psychology.[42]

The difficulty that concerns us primarily, however, is not the ambiguity of research in the behaviorial sciences, but what appears to happen in the differentiation of roles. In present cultures, at least, women in most places have a status inferior to men, and their identity is largely defined in relation to male norms. In Latin, *vir* ("man"; cf. *vis*, "strength") means a male and is identified by its root with "virtue," while *femina* (implying "breast-feeder") means a female. Both are *homo* ("a human being") but, in the Western cultures especially, man is considered to be both *vir* and *homo*, whereas woman is only *femina* and "not quite human."[43] D. H. Lawrence has pointed out that men accept women as anything, except as a human being.

Man is willing to accept woman as an equal, as man in skirts, as an angel, a devil, a baby-face, a machine, an instrument, a bosom, a womb, a pair of legs, a servant, an encyclopaedia, an ideal or an obscenity; the one thing he won't accept her as is a human being, a real human being of the feminine sex.[44]

It is the position of feminists that this objectification of woman's sex role so that it is considered to be her exclusive self-definition is destructive to the full humanity of both women and men. The long androcentric tradition of Hebrew thought and Greek philosophy influenced Western culture and religion to associate man with rational *logos* and heavenly being, and woman with sensuality, passion, and earthly being.[45] In modern times this has led us to think of man as naturally assertive, analytic, and manipulative and woman as interrelated, contextual, wholistic, and we have encultured men and women to fit this masculine-feminine model.[46] In addition, those characteristics and roles associated with men in Western society have been highly rewarded and given prestige, power, and honor, while those associated with women have been regarded as not worthy of economic rewards or social prestige. Marlene Dixon reminds us:

In a society in which money determines value, women are a group who work outside the money economy. Their work is not worth money, is therefore valueless, is therefore not even real work. And women themselves, who do this valueless work, can hardly be expected to be worth as much as men, who work for money.[47]

A feminist approach to the question of sex roles would advocate the freedom to make use of women's abilities, not only in the area of *labor,* which is related to the biological needs of human beings providing the animal necessities, and in *work,* which provides the world of things, but also in the area of *action* (praxis), which is directed toward interaction between people and the creation of world as history. People become subjects as their actions transcend the *labor* of biological necessity and repetitive *work* in order to participate in creating the shape of society.[48] This is why the preponderance of women and Third World people in *labor* and *work* becomes an important issue as part of the development of new male-female roles in society. The feminist approach advocates the freedom to be *different,* not in the sense that male or female must emphasize certain of their cultural characteristics over against each other, but in the sense that each person can grow more whole by developing qualities and economic skills which are at present identified with one or the other sex.[49]

The technological revolution is causing an ongoing *dislocation of life-styles* which has impact on men and women in every country of the globe. The effects of industrialization and urbanization on many societies produce changes in family, economic, and political patterns. These changes are felt in highly developed nations as well as in developing nations. Of particular interest here is the impact of technology on the female biological functions. Already the development of birth control methods has tended to separate sexual intercourse from childbearing. Science is also well on its way to a separation of childbearing from the mother through reproduction of life in test tubes and substitute wombs. In addition, the development of modern medicine and hygiene has resulted in overpopulation so that extensive child-rearing is no longer a necessity for the existence of most societies.

The shifts in life-style related to work and family are not products of a women's revolution, but underlying causes of the search for new forms of meaningful existence. More and more women perceive that their *biology no longer necessarily defines their destiny.* They search for new ways to use their talents because their family and society is often less in need of them as full-time mothers or full-time administrators of agrarian households, and more in need of their full active political-economic participation in the public sector. This leads to a continuing revolution in society which touches not only work and productivity but also basic life-styles related to reproduction, sexuality, and socialization of children.[50]

We have already seen that our actions in shaping the world with others give us human identity. In societies which only value those actions related to *economic productivity,* persons gain a sense of value and worth in proportion to the prestige, income, and power of the job they hold. This fact is causing women and Third World groups to push hard toward equality of opportunity in work situations and to enter the competitive job market as a means of self-liberation. The often repeated white, male injunction to the oppressed that life as an "organization man" is another form of oppression is frequently true. But those who have been relegated to low-paying and nonpaying jobs of labor and work are going to continue to press in this area as long as high-status jobs are the social key to prestige, and self-identity.[51]

Women and men are coming to the recognition that such a system of work and economy is, at root, unjust and needs to be changed. Not only does it maintain an elite at the expense of dehumanization and exploitation of others, but also the "work ethic" in itself is no longer "working."[52] The idea that work is an end in itself, from which we derive meaning, is a secular form of the so-called "Protestant work ethic" which valued work as a means of glorifying God.[53] It is well adapted to an industrial society where time spent in working, organizing, and management is often highly rewarded. However, in a cybernetic world fewer and fewer jobs are available, except in the service industries such as hospitals, schools, hotels, etc. In addition, except for professional and managerial elites, the work available is increasingly meaningless. In such a situation of fewer and fewer jobs, a new economic system and a new work ethic, based on the vocation a person has to service and creativity beyond her or his particular job, are becoming a necessity.

In this shift in society women are caught in the middle. Like other economically disadvantaged groups they are entering the job market at a time of decreasing job opportunities. At the same time the economic pressures which produced the nuclear family, in which a woman is largely isolated from meaningful relationships with other adults, continue to deprive women of a life vocation. Neither childraising nor housework is a full-time or life-time occupation, and the role of the "happy consumer" or sex symbol often is not a satisfying substitute for full use of a woman's talents and energies.[54]

Women have the alternative of seeking out voluntary vocations and they have been well enculturated to find meaning in this new form of "work ethic." Yet, at the moment "volunteerism" is viewed with suspicion as a means of syphoning off the energies of women through preoccupation with "do-goodism" rather than social change.[55] Again the issue seems at root to come back to the need for a new distribution of jobs and vocations so that *both* women and men can find opportunities for creativity, learning, and service in those societies which have increasing time for leisure and fewer jobs available.

The changes brought about by technology have made men and women increasingly aware that new life-styles are also needed in the areas of *family and marriage.* Styles neither of work nor of family life are necessarily changed when women take jobs. At present, in the United States, women make up one third of the labor force, but their increasingly extensive presence has had the net result of their being proportionately more economically disadvantaged than twenty-five years ago.[56] Nor has the fact of full-time employment greatly changed women's role at home. Both in capitalist and communist countries, women usually are expected to hold *two jobs.* They work all day, or all night, and then come home to perform the duties of child care, husband care, and household work.

Women and men are thus beginning to explore alternatives such as communal marriages, serial mating, single parent arrangements, cluster families, polygamy, homosexual arrangements.[57] In the Hebrew-Christian traditions and in various societies, the shape of the family and marriage roles have undergone many different changes over the centuries.[58] To assert that only one arrangement, such as the nuclear family, is possible, is simply to deny the historical and social facts. As Cox indicates:

In the history of biblical religion we have had patriarchy, concubinage, celibacy, group marriage, and serial monogamy. We should not invest monogamy with the sacred significance of being the only legitimate Christian or human form of familial structure.[59]

Those relationships which develop out of new experiments may possibly help men and women to find alternative ways of lasting relationships of full personhood and sustained child care. New forms of human sexuality might provide a basis for new life-styles and roles for women and men, when the experimentation is done, not in response to commercialized eroticism, but out of a deep regard for the partner as a person and subject.[60]

Not Lonesome, but Twosome. If we look at the question of partnership and humanization in the Biblical perspective, we can remind ourselves that women, or for that matter, people, are not necessarily viewed as the *Other*. As we have seen, the Genesis etiological myths are designed to explain the relationship of polarity and attraction between men and women, but their principal focus is on the possibility of reciprocity. Man and woman were created to be in relationship with God and one another. Servanthood, not sexuality, is the primary bearer of God's image. It is only in the myth of the Fall that woman emerges as the *Other* rather than the helper *('ezer)*. In the Yahwist creation story the focus is on the fact that Adam is not supposed to be *lonesome*, but *twosome*.[61] The interpretation of this text, including that of Paul, which asserts that man is to be the head of woman, reflects the social pattern of the ancient world and not necessarily an ontological structure given in creation (I Cor. 11:3–16; Eph. 5:21–33).[62]

When we focus on the meaning of Christ as the Representative it becomes clear that the relationship by which we also become representatives of new humanity is that of servanthood. It is Christ who performed the *first free act* in giving his life *for* many. The freedom of Adam and Eve *from* God and over against each other is a symbol of the old humanity. The new humanity is the beginning of a life that is for God and for others, and, therefore, "twosome" in the deepest sense of the word. Christ's representation means that man and woman are set free *now* to become representatives of that true humanity by working toward new forms of partnership.

In Christ, women and men, oppressed and oppressor, are set free to work together on behalf of the liberating purpose of God. In spite of all its mistakes, and historical evidence to the contrary, the Christian community is called to be a sign of that new humanity where new relationship and life-styles can emerge. Signs of that new beginning can be seen in the early church where both women and men received gifts of the spirit and performed charismatic roles as followers of the *'ebed Yahweh* (Rom. 16:1–2; I Cor. 11:5; 12:4–11).

Present-day authors are also searching for ways by which women can become partners in new life-styles. For instance, Alice Rossi has proposed three possible models that can be applied not only to ethnic groups but also to groups defined by race or sex.[63] The models come out of her studies of current sociological concepts of acculturation into a dominant culture. They provide a typology of alternative forms of cooperation.

The *pluralistic model* anticipates a society in which differences are retained in a heterogenous form. The problem of this model is that it serves to perpetuate segregation with blacks in unskilled jobs and segregated schools and neighbor-hoods. For women it reinforces traditional sex-role stereo-types rather than challenging them.

The *assimilation model* assumes that in time the op-pressed group will be absorbed into the mainstream of so-ciety. The problem of this model is that it assumes that women will become equal by gaining equal places in the occupational and political sector. This will not be a possibility as long as women are still expected to be the supporters of men in their exclusively economic role, and, therefore, to carry two jobs. Another danger is that it assumes the model of the dominant group as the best one; only women's roles need to change in order for them to "fit."

The *hybrid model*, which Rossi advocates, rejects tradi-tional psychological assumptions about sex roles, and inher-ited institutional structures. It calls for a new society in which "the lives of men and whites will be different, not only women and blacks."[64] Such a model can come about only through coalitions of youth, women, social activists, and Third World people consciously seeking out a new identity and searching for new structures that can help both the op-pressed and the oppressor move toward a fuller life. Only in this way can the "woman's question" become the "man's question" and so the "human question" as women and men become *twosome* in seeking to fulfill their common destiny.[65]

The praxis of liberation theology can assist in working out such social patterns that try to overcome human dislocation and oppression. Impelled by the call of God's Representative to become representatives of a newly human society, it strug-gles to find the way toward partnership, identity, and future for all humankind.

6: COMMUNION IN DIALOGUE

The vision of new humankind where there is true partner-ship is hard to actualize in a world in which hierarchical structures dominate our lives. Such structures are painfully present, not only in politics, economics, and family but also in the church—the very community that is called to be a sign of partnership and humanization. The church oppresses the lives of Third World people by legitimatizing the status quo and helping to support white, Western imperialism. It op-presses the lives of the laity by perpetuating a clerical caste system that dominates the affairs of most confessional bodies and inhibits participation of all believers. It oppresses the lives of women by excluding them from decision-making and equality, and endorsing the cultural myths of their ontologi-cal inferiority. Small wonder, then, that liberation theologies have a tendency to number the church among the oppres-sors, and to speak of it mainly as an institution *from* which we must be liberated!

Liberation theologians, however, need to work together with others to set the church free *for* its true calling to participate in God's Mission in the world. Regardless of its particular ecclesiastical organization, the center of a Chris-tian community is the person and presence of Christ, who promises to be with his people wherever they gather to call upon his name (Matt. 18:20). Where Christ is, there is the church, and there also is freedom. This freedom has to be actualized in helping people hear the word of the gospel and begin to live it out among themselves and with and for others.

The structures of the church are often *heretical structures* that prevent the word from being heard and shared so that it becomes a blessing for others. Those forms of organization which stand in the way of God's Mission have to be subjected to a searching analysis so that they can be replaced or supplemented in order to help the church become a sign of God's intended future.[1] Liberation theologians cannot ignore this task of *subverting the church into being the church,* if they are to be faithful to the One who calls them into community and solidarity with others. Focusing on the concerns of the oppressed can help to guard against "interior decoration" and provide an opportunity for radical critique and the opening up of the church for its task in the world.

Liberation theologies cannot abandon the church because it is in the community of faith that the praxis of theology is nurtured. As men and women seek to reflect on the events of the world in the light of God's actions, they need a community of faith and witness. Otherwise, theology itself fails to be praxis and takes on a hierarchical structure in which truths are "handed down from above" by those who are supposed to know better. Thomas O'Meara reminds us that the direction and dynamics of theology itself needs to be reversed, "so that not only the questions are given by the situation of crisis, but the theological response is the effect of the experience of action and ministry."[2]

The community of faith is one of the *loci* for trying to find ways to actualize the signs of new humanity now. This is a possibility because Christ's presence with his people creates *koinōnia* in their midst. The word *koinōnia* is usually translated by the words "communion," "participation," "fellowship," "sharing." It is an indication of the presence of *shalom* as seen in a close relationship with someone or a sharing together in something.[3] Communion is *participation with*

Christ in his work as the representative of God's love to others, and *sharing with his community* in common actions of celebration, reflection, and service in the world (I Cor. 10:16–17).

This communion, or participation, is dialogical in nature. It assumes that the togetherness of human beings with God in Christ and with others is part of becoming truly human. Dialogue is made possible because God speaks to us and comes to be with us through the Holy Spirit. In return, we can respond to God and one another in shared words, emotions, and obedient actions. And because we can communicate with one another, we enter into a relationship of communion.

Paulo Freire has described dialogue as *encounter between people mediated by the world in order to name the world.*[4] Such dialogue is difficult, if not impossible, between oppressor and oppressed because there is no genuine encounter between people when all the power and authority flows one way. Nor is there likely to be any shared world view or common desire for change of the status quo. But in the Christian community new forms of dialogue might make communion or participation possible.

In order to investigate this "possible impossibility" we need to look at a plausible context for participation and partnership through *open ecclesiology* and then to investigate ways of entering into *dialogue* with *all* people of the First, Second, Third, and Fourth Worlds. In conclusion it is important to look at ways in which all those who call on Christ's name can find their way to *participation in ministry* as representatives of the One who came "not to be served but to serve" (Mark 10:45).

OPEN ECCLESIOLOGY

There are many perspectives on ecclesiology, but when the missionary nature of the church as God's representative in the world is the chosen perspective, this leads to what is sometimes called *open ecclesiology*.[5] This is an open-ended view of ecclesiology which investigates the variety of possible shapes the church might take in order to participate in God's traditioning activity. It is a marked change in the method of doing ecclesiology. Previously theologians tended to begin with the nature of the church and argued from its nature to its function. Open ecclesiology begins with the function of participation and moves from there to understanding the form and nature of the church.

This change is characterized by Colin Williams as a "radical shift in focus" from direct to indirect ecclesiology.[6] The direct focus ceases to be on the church, and is on God and the world. The church only indirectly comes into focus as a postscript on that reality. One way of expressing this is to say that the church is seen as a P.S. on God's love affair with the world (John 3:16). The study of the Missionary Structure of the Congregation by the World Council of Churches has pointed out that the renewal of the church begins with a perspective that moves from God's sending activity (the *missio Dei*), to the address of God's sending activity (the *world*), and finally to the transitory forms of obedience to that sending (the *church*). Such a perspective is one of *God-World-Church*, and not *God-Church-World*.[7]

God's action in the *polis* (society) sets women and men free to join Christ in representing what it means to be human. In this light it is possible to speak of the church as *a theopolitical event of liberation toward new humanity*. Participation in this event involves service to others through actions that anticipate God's intended future. The church is called to become *open to the world, to others,* and *to the future*.

Open to the World. The church has no walls, nor does it draw a circle around itself that separates it from the world. The community of faith forms an "open circle" around its center: the presence of Jesus Christ. The circle should be open enough for other people to see and join in the central Christ event (I Cor. 14:13–19). It should also be open enough for the congregation to move out from the center to see and join in the Christ event with others wherever it happens in the world. Those who have been called by Christ are only separate from the world in order to be prepared for this engagement with the world. In this sense the *Church for Others* speaks of the church as *pars pro toto* (a part for the whole).

The church lives in order that the world may know its true being. It is *pars pro toto;* it must live "ex-centredly." It has to seek out those situations in the world that call for living responsibility and there it must announce and point to *shalom.*[8]

Thus the church is seen, not as a religious assembly, temple, synagogue, or sect which is closed or sacred, but as a part of the world where it joins God's action in becoming a pressure group for change. It appears that in seeking to convey the openness of the new Christian communities in contrast to the restricted Jewish communities, Paul and others working with Gentiles used the word *ekklēsia* to describe the gatherings of Christians.[9] In non-Biblical Greek this word referred to "political" assemblies and could thus be used in a *theopolitical* sense to describe the new people of God (Acts 19:32, 39–41). In the same way the word "Christian" was probably coined as a secular word to refer to the Christians as a "political" group associated with Christ (Acts 11:26).

The usage of the word *ekklēsia* reflects its functional character. It refers to the totality of Christians living in any one place—a city or a house (I Cor. 1:2; 16:19). It also refers to the church universal in which all believers belong as part of the eschatological people of God (I Cor. 12:28). These communities were defined simply by the presence of Christ in their midst and viewed their task as that of witnessing to the gospel.[10] Just such functional character is stressed by Barth in his *Church Dogmatics* as he points out that the task of the church is mission; the proclamation of the gospel to the world.[11]

Open to Others. Because open ecclesiology is *theocentric* and not *ecclesiocentric* it is concerned with all people. Its focus is on being together with other women and men as a manifestation of the humanity of God. Those who in past ecclesiastical traditions have been described as *Others* are no longer "outside" the church which is an open circle.

The *Others* who were "separated brethren" find that they belong together as "dearly beloved brethren" in the work of representing Christ in the world, in spite of their denominational affiliation. There is one call and one pilgrimage in Mission, yet from the beginnings of the church there have always been varieties in the way that pilgrimage was to be lived and carried out. In spite of this variety, members of Christ's church express their unity by opening themselves to each other's different ways of following Christ.

The *Others* who are men and women of "living faiths and ideologies" are also seen as included in God's purpose and care.[12] The problem of relating to other religions and to ideologies is crucial in a world society bound together by economic interdependence, rapid communication and travel, and the common threat of war.[13] It is an issue that no liberation theology can ignore if it is to confront the situations of human division in a world united in one common history.

This raises the question of the relation of salvation to the presence of the church. Its classical formulation by Origen, Cyprian, and others in their formulation of *no salvation outside the church (extra ecclesiam nulla salus)* declared that no one could be saved except by Christ and that the *locus* of that salvation was Christ's church. The formulation of this axiom goes back to the image of the church as the ark of Noah (I Peter 3:20). Peter says that there is salvation, through baptism, inside the ark, but does not assert that there is none outside.[14] In a situation of world religions and ideologies the idea of the church as the exclusive means of salvation has been increasingly under attack. In recent thinking, the church is more often seen as the "extraordinary means of salvation," or as one of the means by which God's salvific will is accomplished.[15] The shift is toward a new imagery in which the church is seen more in the metaphor of the *rainbow* in Gen. 9:12–13.

And God said, "This is the sign of the covenant which I make between me and you and every living creature that is with you, for all future generations. I set my bow in the cloud, and it shall be a sign of the covenant between me and the earth."

The church is one of the signs of cosmic salvation and not the exclusive mediator of that salvation.[16]

In general there are two ways of describing this shift to open ecclesiology in current discussions. The first is that of *wider ecumenism,* represented in the teachings of Vatican II, especially in *Lumen Gentium.*[17] The Roman Catholic Church is pictured at the center of expanding concentric circles or zones which situate all of humankind in some kind of relationship to the center circle and to Christ. It can be said that there is *no salvation outside the church* because all members of the human race are somehow related to the Roman Catholic Church which stands as the universal sign and sacrament of salvation.[18]

An alternative way would be to speak of *open ecumenism* in which the church is also seen as a participant in God's salvation for humanity. This view has been spelled out by Hans Küng as well as by many Protestant theologians. In their argument there is *no salvation outside of Christ,* who is God's representative of the new humanity. In Christ the world has been redeemed. God has already elected all people to enjoy the fruits of the plan of salvation.[19] The church is simply that part of the world which calls upon the name of Christ, and points to God's concern for all people by sharing in Christ's election for service. The Christian community, as it appears in *diaspora*, is found where Christ's presence is recognized, but it has no walls that separate it from others; only a center in the person of Christ.

Whatever nomenclature is used, that of wider ecumenism, or open ecumenism, or some other, it is clear, as Küng describes it, that the church is open to others because it represents a radical universalism that is grounded in Jesus Christ.

Every human being is under God's grace and can be saved: . . . and we may hope that everyone is.
Every world religion is under God's grace and can be a way of salvation . . . and we may hope that every one is.[20]

Open to the Future. Open ecclesiology is always provisional and in search of new structures because it is open to what may happen in the future. As Moltmann has reminded us, the nature of the church as an "Exodus community" has to be taken seriously.[21] It constantly moves and changes, not simply in response to the whim of a changing world, but in response to its calling to work and live by the promises of God who works in and through history. It exists to actualize *shalom* by concrete actions for justice, peace, and wholeness, and responds to its calling to be a community that lives, not by the standards of the world, nor of the past, but by the memory of hope. In Ruether's description:

The Church should relate to society, not by being co-opted by it to sanctify the *status quo,* nor simply withdraw from it in isolated purity, but rather the proper relationship of the Church to society is dialectical. The Church should stand in the midst of conventional society, but not be "of it," but rather be the place where a significantly new humanity, functioning in a communitarian and non-exploitive way, is begun.[22]

Openness to the future is an indication that a Christian community has already experienced the liberating presence of the new creation in Jesus Christ. As *pars pro toto*, the church lives on behalf of the future of humanity and thus seeks to live "as if" that future were already here. This stance leads, not only to open ecumenism but also to the *proleptic* or *anticipatory ecumenism* that shares both the groanings and the liberation of society in anticipation of the time that all "nations" will come to God's banquet (Isa. 25:6–8). A proleptic sign of this openness to the future is the act of participation or communion together in the Lord's Supper which "proclaims the Lord's death until he comes" (I Cor. 11:26). Such a community seeks to show forth that intended future by already refusing, now, to be defined by age, sex, color, or ethnicity, and by becoming "those who know pain and want to share it" because they have tasted the *apéritif* of freedom in the midst of suffering.[23]

DIALOGUE: IMPOSSIBLE POSSIBILITY

Open ecclesiology depends on dialogue as a praxis of freedom because there can be little openness for the world without common solidarity in suffering and alienation, and willingness to work for change. There can be little openness to others without humility about one's own position, and trust in the integrity and value of the persons and groups involved. There can be little openness for the future apart from shared hope in the possibility of a new human society.

Encounter between people is also important to community in the church that is based on joint participation in the shared life-style of Jesus of Nazareth. It becomes impossible when certain few do all the talking and acting. Dialogue is a key to community with women and men of living faiths and ideologies which is based on mutual trust and shared concern for the unified world in which we live. It becomes impossible when the representatives of Christian "servanthood" are perceived as propagandists and oppressors.

If we take even a casual look at churches as they exist

today, dialogue appears to be an impossibility. Distinctions of ecclesiastical rank, sex, race, and class appear to render churches into "zones of monologue." The same dismal view is to be seen in society where economic, political, national, and racial divisions render the bonding in community to transform the world an impossibility.

This cannot be the last word, however, for those working toward new humanity. There are ways in which we can *begin* to act and reflect together. There are ways in which the oppressors and oppressed can try to move toward what Rossi calls a *hybrid* society or community, with new configurations of social interaction. There are also ways in which oppressed and silent groups can learn to bond together in naming and changing the world according to their own perceptions of the meaning of freedom.

Christians believe that it is possible for the church to be open, and for dialogue and community to happen. This is a *possible impossibility* because God has entered into dialogue with us so that we may learn to name and transform the world. It is possible because Christ has become the representative of *all* humanity, and places us together *with* each other. Therefore, it is important to investigate the *forms of dialogue* that are being developed in pursuit of an openness to others that strives to break down the barriers of mutual distrust. At the same time, we need to look carefully at dialogue among the *oppressors and oppressed,* and consider ways to overcome both vertical violence between the two groups and horizontal violence between members of oppressed groups.

Forms of Dialogue. Can a white "think black"? Can a Christian "think Buddhist"? Can the rich "think poor"? Can a man "think woman"? This sort of impossibility has been suggested by Lawrence Howard, himself an Afro-American, in reference to thinking black.

Black consciousness is open to anyone who in the present turmoil now facing the nation will operate in terms of black categories. . . . Blacks, in the deepest sense, are people of any color who are dedicated to emancipation, national interdependence, freedom from fear and human fulfillment—whose priority is always people over property or machines. Blacks are all those who affirm the species in its deepest psychic dimensions.[24]

Analyzing this statement, we discover that it is possible to "think black, or Buddhist, or poor, or woman." Possible, because we share a common humanity and can learn to move beyond *identity* toward *mutuality*. At the same time we realize that it is impossible, literally to enter into the life of another person or group completely. Mutuality means that one shares consciousness and trust, not that one becomes identical with the other person. Forms of dialogue are designed by those who want to further this process of sharing and mutuality. They represent more a style of living and thinking than simply an exchange of words.[25]

There are many suggested lists which have been drawn up by those concerned with spelling out the guidelines for dialogue. In the field of theology one would think, for instance, of the writings of Paul Tillich, Robert McAfee Brown, Vatican II, the World Council of Churches, and "evangelical" groups concerned with the difference between evangelism and dialogue.[26] These guidelines speak of the conviction, trust, knowledge, humility, openness, etc. Each list is always partial because the forms of dialogue vary with each circumstance. If we focus on how people actually enter into dialogue, it is possible, however, to suggest at least three models of dialogue which are presently being explored and tested in a variety of situations: mutual interpellation, dialogical action, and shared world.

Mutual interpellation is a style of thinking your way together into action. Here groups are willing to risk change and new ideas by joining together in dialogue around a common theme or need for change in society. This mode of dialogue has proved helpful, especially in recent Marxist-Christian discussions which have taken place in Europe and the Third World.[27] Jan Lochmann has suggested that in mutual interpellation, or challenging one another's positions, a service is done for the other party by emphasizing one's own position in order to help the other group to awaken to an awareness of the shortcomings of its position.[28] For instance, the interpretation of Marxism to Christians can help the latter to become more attentive to immanence instead of emphasizing metaphysics and privatized inwardness. The interpretation of Christianity to Marxists might help the latter to become more attentive to the transcendence of hope as a genuine human dimension.

In a similar fashion women and men can learn to think their way into new actions and cooperative life-styles, if they begin with agreement on the need for basic social changes and examine one another's perspectives to find out ways of moving ahead together. The problem here is getting from discussion into action.

For this reason a more useful mode of dialogue between groups might be that of *dialogical action.* Here women and men act their way into thinking together. Through an agreed-upon agenda of action, people sometimes find that they can move beyond their own prejudices. Those of different faiths or races or classes can find unity in dialogical action as they work together in the Third World as partners in "nation-building." White people can learn to overcome the prejudice against blacks that infects United States society by joining in a common project such as housing renewal or education reform. Women and men can begin by making coalitions to change wages and working conditions, political structures, or laws governing divorce and abortion. Out of this common agenda of action new attitudes toward the problems of men and women in society may develop.

Shared world is a mode of dialogue in which people can

not only think and act but also experience the same environment together. People begin to share words when they are sharing world. Today such sharing often comes about naturally because of the pluralistic makeup of the society where people live. Sharing is carried out intentionally by such projects as those of the World Council of Churches in dialogue centers in Asia.[29] It is also the most obvious form of dialogue between men and women and has great potential for new life-styles and partnership in marriage and work, where there is intentional and contractual formation of a process of learning by living together.

Oppressor and Oppressed. Dialogue implies a desire and an ability to move toward mutuality and trust. It becomes hard in a hierarchical situation in which one group insists on naming or describing reality on its own, and impossible, when that party has the power to force the *Others* to accept the world named and defined by the dominant group. Dialogue cannot even take place when there is no encounter between people, mediated by the world, to name and transform it. Such a situation is one of *vertical violence* in which social, psychological, and physical violence is exerted against the oppressed. Those who are the victims of this vertical violence also find it difficult to enter into dialogue with each other because of the dynamic of *horizontal violence* which is at work to undercut their relationship to one another.

In order to move together in the dialectic of liberation, toward new awareness and ability to act, it is important to remember that the use of the words "oppressor" and "oppressed" is not necessarily directed at particular individuals who happen by accident of birth to belong to an oppressing group. The discussion is not *ad personam* (about the person), but *ad rem* (about the thing); that is, about the fabric of society in which people are locked into various forms of oppression in a vicious circle that dehumanizes both the oppressor and the oppressed. It is an attempt to describe the world in such a way that this sickness can be confronted and changed.

The oppressed, of course, are not necessarily the "virtuous" ones who are always right. The danger they risk in struggling to transform the world is that of adopting an ideology which asserts that they will automatically become virtuous rulers over others, should they come to power. Our gaze must constantly be focused on ways of changing the hierarchical structure of society and not simply raising up a new set of oppressors.[30] Thus the revolution has to be an ongoing struggle, both against ourselves and "the principalities and powers."

The gospel of liberation is for *all* people. Christ died for "the many," and that includes all classes and groups in society. God has a special concern for the oppressed because they are usually the ones most in need of liberation. Yet Jesus ate with those viewed as quislings, servants of the Roman oppressors, and even called a tax collector to be his disciple (Luke 18:10-14; 19:1-10; Matt. 9:9). He judged the religious rulers of his time, not because they were not in need of help, but because this is the help they needed. Those who claim that only the poor or suffering are loved by God are tending to make this into another form of "works' righteousness" by which to earn God's love.

This does not discount the fact that forms of *vertical violence* exercised by the oppressors are indeed violations of justice, freedom, and dignity. In this situation, it is the oppressed who, in freeing themselves, make possible a new society in which such freedom can be shared with all people. Liberation is a priority, which, nevertheless, must also move toward reconciliation in the process of searching out new human dignity.[31] In the first stage, according to Freire,

... the oppressed unveil the world of oppression and through the praxis commit themselves to its transformation. In the second stage, in which the reality of oppression has already been transformed, this pedagogy ceases to belong to the oppressed and becomes a pedagogy of all . . . [people] in the process of permanent liberation.[32]

Having initiated violence by their use of power, privilege, and manipulation, the oppressors call forth the counterviolence and struggle by which the oppressed strive to free themselves, and to help to free their oppressors as well. Out of this situation can come a moment in which both groups are willing to "share world" and a new humanity emerges which is "neither oppressor, nor oppressed, but man [and woman] in the process of liberation."[33]

In working toward a possibility of dialogue, *what is it that the oppressor can do?* This is a problem that confronts most of us at one time or another, when we find ourselves in the position of dehumanizing others.

First, members of oppressing groups can *trust the oppressed* to work for liberation, and to decide when they have been empowered.[34] It is not enough just to give away power, because the ones who receive power as a gift know that it probably can be taken back again. Nor can the oppressors play the role of deciding when they think the oppressed have made enough gains and should be "quiet." Liberation is a process of self-liberation in community with others. The recognition of this fact is essential to anyone who wishes to work with the oppressed.

Second, the people of the oppressor group can learn to play a *support role* in working with those who are struggling to liberate themselves, and trusting in their ability to take the lead. This is often hard to do for those who are used to providing leadership and to "having all the answers," but it is essential if they are to join in the common human struggle. To put it bluntly, with J. Deotis Roberts,

. . . as far as blacks are concerned, whites may no longer be lieutenants but buck privates in the black community. They, however, may work at full potential in their own community to prepare their white neighbors for accepting blacks as people in a pluralistic or multiracial society.[35]

Third, oppressors can become *advocates,* helping to break barriers in the society. This calls for the risk of moving from a stance of *liberalism* to *liberation,* in which those who have leverage for change are willing to work, using political power as advocates with and for others.[36] At the very least, someone who wishes to advocate the cause of another group can "get out of the way," in order to let the others have "room to breathe" and positions of new authority.

Fourth, persons of oppressed groups can learn to understand the things which oppress their own lives, and begin their own process of *conscientization;* moving to understand their own identity and history.[37] This is why men's liberation groups and white consciousness-raising groups play a vital part in the total process of overcoming the vertical violence of sexism and racism. In this consciousness-raising process, the oppressors also go through their own dialectic of liberation.

They move from a prior stage of opposition, ridicule, jokes, or apathy to what Peter L. Kranz calls the stage of the white (or male, or Western) *expert* who manages to continue to keep verbal distance by "having all the answers."[38] As members of the oppressor group become more involved, they reach the *armor* stage of defensiveness in which they refuse to let the *Others* "tell it like it is," and retreat behind a smoke screen of side issues and points of order. The *soul* stage is reached when the oppressors begin to perceive their own identity and the causes of their defensiveness and inhuman existence. Finally the stage might be reached of *self-acceptance* or positive social identity, in which members of the oppressor group are willing to challenge the structures of their own communities and join in the work to change the status quo. Although Kranz uses these terms to describe the stages of conscientization for middle-class whites, they are very similar in the struggles of men against sexism or of non-Third World people against political, economic, and cultural imperialism.

The same questions can be asked of the oppressed, as well as the oppressors. *What can they do* to work toward dialogue as a *praxis* of freedom? We have already examined the process of conscientization for the oppressed, but it is important to focus on a principal barrier to dialogue; that of *horizontal violence.* Oppressed groups have internalized the consciousness of the oppressor as a *false consciousness.*[39] They have been taught to believe in a reality that alienates them and justifies their oppression. Therefore, they tend to think of themselves as inferior, uneducated, undependable, etc. The frustrations that arise in this situation cause the oppressed to take out their aggression, not on the oppressor, but on the only safe victims: the others who are oppressed.

At the very moment when dialogue is a key factor in the process of bonding and conscientization, the dynamics of oppression turn the oppressed against each other. This dynamic is well known to the oppressors who make use of it at every turn as a means of control. At the very least, they continue to subvert the process of conscientization by encouraging Third World and Fourth World groups to adjust to their situation through such methods as psychotherapy and group encounter.[40]

The forms of dialogue that may be helpful in a situation of equals who share agenda and trust sometimes become counterproductive among oppressed people through the dynamics of horizontal violence. In the process of *mutual interpellation* among women or blacks, there turns out to be a great deal said, including gossiping, "put down," "cover up," which focuses on infighting and prevents creative dialogue with the world that needs change.[41] The process of *dialogical action* is often prevented because of the long history of oppressed groups who are divided and conquered. Instead of

bonding together in sisterhood and brotherhood the oppressed fight against each other, functioning, not as teams,
but as "kings" and "queens," staking out their own small
piece of "turf" in emulation of the oppressor.[42] The *sharing
of world* cannot lead to dialogue if it is in an airtight ghet-
toized world or prison, not open to the wider society. In such
a situation horizontal violence against one another can lead
to blacks destroying their own communities or to women
taking out their own neuroses on each other and their families.[43]

The building of community and dialogue can only begin
when we take seriously the understanding of salvation and
liberation as a social as well as an individual event, and begin
to deal with all the various social dynamics that are obstacles
to communication. In dialogue with those who oppress, vertical violence must be understood and overcome in all its psychological and social ramifications. In dialogue within or between oppressed groups, horizontal violence must be dealt
with in the building of new community. Liberation theology
invites us to take part in this task, asking us to work toward
the possible impossibility of community so that one day people will begin to say, "What if they gave a revolution and
everybody won?"[44]

PARTICIPATION IN MINISTRY

The search for communion and dialogue between equals
has direct ramifications for the racism, sexism, and classism
that exist in present-day church structures. In order to look
more specifically at one aspect of this problem, it is important
to examine the question of clerical ordination and its antidia-
logical effect on women and on the whole ministry of the
people *(laos)* of God. This particular aspect is symbolic of the
oppressive structures of church life. It is also a key issue in the
struggle of Christian women to find a dynamic sisterhood
among themselves and with all women that might help to

renew the life of the church for its mission of liberation and reconciliation. This was pointed out by the first women's caucus at the General Assembly of the National Council of the Churches of Christ in 1969.

You cannot seriously undertake the quest for meaning and wholeness called for in the Mission in the '70s Report unless you are willing to deal with the role of women. "Search for community in a modern secular society" will be futile if we do not now face up to what it means that God created human life in *our* image—male and female.[45]

In the church, women and men "share world" together. In the light of the one ministry of Jesus Christ in which both are called to participate, the question ought not to arise, Why should *women* be ordained as clergy? They are already a part of those who have inherited Christ's ministry of suffering service (Mark 10:43–45; I Peter 4:10). The question ought to arise, Why should *men* or anyone else be ordained to a special clerical status when all share the one calling of the whole people? Perhaps the monologue which has replaced dialogue in many Christian communities is partly caused by this stratification of the body of Christ so that it is no longer able to speak the word, and name the world in genuine communion.

Problem of Ministry. The understanding and practice of ministry has been a problem in the life of Christian churches for some time. Changes in the structure of society and the church have brought with them ever-changing roles. Identity crises are common among clergy of all confessions who try to interpret their calling in the light of personal and ecclesial needs.[46] Personal and institutional financial crises result in personal insecurity and anxiety as job openings become less available.

Such problems are compounded by women engaged in ministry. As more and more women of all confessions seek education that will prepare them for clerical ordination, the old roles of male clergy appear even more restrictive and inadequate.[47] Pressure on the job market by women, who are beginning to constitute as much as 30 percent of theological seminary enrollment, is a threat not only to the churches who refuse to ordain women but also to those who have no job openings for them when they graduate. Renewal in religious communities leads to a broadened image of apostolic ministry which sometimes brings conflict with the hierarchy.

These problems are further complicated by the anachronistic understanding of clerical ordination that exists in practice, if not in theory, in most churches as they continue to be male dominated on the local, national, and international levels. Pressure for the liberation of women in societies around the world is slowly exposing the sexist practices of church life, language, and organization. A persistent chorus of voices, both female and male, is calling for a new look at the meaning of ministry and mission in a world calling out for justice and liberation for all people.

It is rather easy to describe the meaning of ministry in terms of Jesus' servanthood. But ministry raises a problem for women who wish to serve in the contemporary church. Ministry has been identified with an *all-male caste system* that dominates the work of most churches. This raises many questions for those considering ordination or service in a variety of church ministries.[48] For many people this form of status seems dysfunctional in the modern, more democratic structures of society.

The question of clerical ordination has been widely investigated in every theological discipline as well as in related social sciences.[49] A minimal ecumenical consensus seems to have been reached on certain points. These, however, do not have much actual effect on ordination practices. There is agreement that the ministries of the church are derivative from Christ in his threefold function of Prophet, Priest, and King. This is known as the *triplex munus.*[50] There is also agreement that this ministry is the calling of the whole people of God, although only certain people are set apart by clerical ordination.[51] Lastly, there is agreement that the New Testament reflects a varied pattern of ministry: president and deacon in the Pauline churches that recognized a wide variety of *charismata* among those who followed the lifestyle of the *'ebed Yahweh* as apostles, prophets, teachers, and deacons, but did not practice ordination; and presbyter (elder) in the Palestinian churches which practiced ordination (I Cor. 12:4–11; Eph. 4:1–16; Acts 14:23; 15:2; 20:17).[52]

These functions of ministry initially were not *orders*, but flexible means of carrying out the mission and work of the church. There is no clear consensus on how many of these functions were performed by women, but it seems probable that women received the gifts of the Spirit and exercised charismatic or *evangelizing* ministries, although they tended to be barred from the *administrative* role because this role seems to have been viewed as a continuation of the male role of "elder" in Jewish tradition.[53] At any rate the early church had no concept of authoritarian ministry because the model was that of *diakonia*. The male priesthood of the Old Testament was seen as fulfilled in Jesus Christ, the high priest. The identification of a *cultual* role with priesthood is a later development (Heb. 7:26–28; I Peter 2:9).[54]

As the early catholic tradition developed, there were many extra-catholic groups that refused to conform to the masculinization of church ministries. Some early sects such as the Montanists had women leaders who claimed the right to be priests and bishops on the basis of Gal. 3:28.[55] In the process of institutionalization of the church a consolidation of functions occurred in which the bishop as the chief pastor of the local church came to represent the fullness of the ministry, assisted by presbyters (priests), and deacons. The charismatic ministries declined and gradually the various types of ministries were formed into an ascending hierarchy of orders parallel to the existing organization of the Roman imperial society.[56]

Traditional approaches to the meaning of ordination reflect particular ecclesial positions. Those who consider the priesthood to be of the *esse* (or being) of the church tend to suggest the restriction of ordination to the sacramental and pastoral role, possibly extending it to deacons or older men, and to those without theological training in places of severe shortage.[57] Those who consider ministry to be the church's *plene esse* (necessary to the fullness of the church) or its *bene esse* (necessary to the well-being of the church) tend to suggest the broadening of ordination to many walks of life, and to the so-called "specialized ministries."[58] There are others, of course, who consider ministry in its present form to be the church's *male esse* (bad for the life, renewal, and mission of the church) and tend to call for a new look at the way women and men are set aside for Christ's service.

The positions of women on the issue of ordination are as varied as those of the various confessional groups.[59] The women who are ordained or seeking ordination do agree, however, in their conviction that it is essential that all the ministries of the church include both women and men. The strategies which they use concerning the question of ordination for women depend on the tradition within which they are working and on the immediate problems faced.

Those who still face the *exclusion* of women from ordination are pushing hard to translate the "theologians' consensus" that nothing prevents it, into a "political consensus" that women have no defect that bars them from sharing with men in the tasks of ministry.[60] One of the problems of this position appears to be that some women have a tendency to buy into the clerical system rather than to demand transformation of the understanding of ministry so that men and women would have more creative roles to fulfill in the mission of the church. On the other hand, many women who may not wish to be ordained are often found among those who think "that it is the whole concept of priesthood which must be rethought."[61]

Those who face *de facto exclusion* of women from pastoral

ministry as a result of lack of jobs are working on task forces, commissions, and committees such as those in the United Church of Christ, The United Methodist Church, and The United Presbyterian Church U.S.A., seeking to enforce equal hiring practices at all levels of church life. Difficulties in this area are presented by the contracting job market that incre⸱ses the hostility of male clergy and slows down the process ⸱f change. In these situations women sometimes also face the opposition of volunteer women who do not yet see the importance of shared power and responsibility on every level of church life.

Some women have long since grown disillusioned with the whole system of ordination as it is now practiced. They consider it to be *dysfunctional* for the reasons we have already discussed, and are pushing for new understanding of pluralized ministries of shorter duration which could include people from all walks of life. These women tend to see ordination as a perpetuation of a male caste system which must be transformed in order for women to receive equal recognition and use of their gifts of the Spirit. The problem here is that such a change would mean radical renewal of the structures of church life at a time when the mood of the church seems to be one of retreat and consolidation.

There are also a growing number of women who have simply decided to *drop out* of the organized church structures altogether. They tend to look for alternative forms of community that allow sisterhood to flower without the restraints of male-dominated bureaucracies.[62] Those who take this position help to create breathing space for their sisters working within the organized church by their more radical stance from the outside. However, their position also raises the question of the loss of a power base within the church. They leave to others the work of raising the consciousness of the vast majority of women who are church members and do have the power of numbers to transform the church for its mission in the world.

Having looked at the varieties of positions that appear to

be available to women at the present moment in working for changes in the understanding of ordination, we must remember that such a typology is only for the sake of analysis and understanding. In real life women find themselves in two or three categories at the same time. It is clear, however, that there is a growing number of women who are concerned about the ministry and mission of the church and the ways in which it can more fully represent a partnership of men and women in service.

Models of Ministry. If we adopt the stance that the form of ministry of the church is derivative from its function as a participant in God's Mission or traditioning action, it follows that there will be many models of ministry, both within one Christian community and across the world. The ministry of representation of true humanity will be situation-variable; taking form according to the needs of each situation. This work will not be the exclusive province of a small group of male clergy, but will be the concern of all the people of God as they join with others in working for liberation and blessing in today's world.

In some cases, the models that are most suited to a particular mission will be those developed over the years of church tradition. In other cases, new models need to be developed that are more adequately suited to open ecclesiology and to the emerging future of church and society. No one can prescribe the shape of the ministry for each situation, but it might help us to look briefly at the models available to us from the past and those emerging in the present changing situation.

As we have seen, the medieval church identified its models of ministry with status and thought of the variety of orders as a succession of offices. The three most important models of ministry in this period were that of *bishop, priest,* and *monk.* The *theologian* was also a model that developed separately out of the old guild structure of the university, although the theologians were usually also part of a monastic order or connected to a cathedral or church.[63] The Reformation showed a great concern and interest in an educated clergy. Stress on the Bible and on the preached word led to the creation of schools at all levels to train laity in reading and to prepare clergy for their role as servants of the Word of God.[64] The model of ministry for the Calvinists became the *praeceptor,* one who exercised discipline in the congregation as a learned minister. The Lutheran model was that of *preacher* whose pastoral role was related to the importance of the proclaimed Word. The Anglican model tended to follow that of bishop, priest, and monk, although the other Protestant models were also put forward during the seventeenth century. In the eighteenth century the beginnings of evangelical awakening and piety brought with it the emergence of the model of ministry as *evangelist.*

In the modern era the churches have sought to adjust their models of ministry to the process of secularization. On the American scene, as denominations emerged in the nineteenth century, seminaries were begun to assure a continued supply of theologically educated clergy for the expanding work of the churches. In the twentieth century the model of learned ministry has given way to a number of variations, the most important of which is that of *professional ministry.* Another variation of learned ministry was one suggested by H. Richard Niebuhr as the *pastoral director* who was not only theologically competent, but also able to function in the administration of the modern churches. A third suggestion has been that of a model of *Christian ministries,* with students receiving training that emphasizes growth, maturity, and flexibility in order to fit into the framework of a pluralistic society.[65]

The difficulty with these models is that they all still follow the older forms, designing only variations that do not get at the root of the problem. First, they begin with the question of *ministry,* and try to train people to fit into that model, rather than asking the question of *mission,* and of how to educate people to involve themselves in the many and changing patterns that are needed. Second, they try to move more and more toward specialized, professional ministries, neglecting the idea that ministry is one of servanthood. This professional model perpetuates and enlarges the distance between professionals and "clients," rather than working to eliminate the clergy line. Lastly, the models are largely based on the presupposition that the people entering the ministry will be white, middle-class, males.

Any *new models of ministry* developed from the perspective of open ecclesiology would have to begin from God's Mission of liberation in the world. Such models would thus stress the importance of learning as a continuing participation in action (service) and reflection (doing theology). They would move toward such a variety of specialization that ministers would not be professional clergy, but those involved in servanthood who have many different professional and nonprofessional skills which are needed in today's world. New models would begin with the assumption that all the people of God are ministers, and each one needs help in finding ways to develop his or her gifts for service. And, of course, they would grow out of the premise that women and Third World people would assume roles of competence in proportion to their numbers in the church and societies where they serve. The "laying on of hands" would not set apart only those with certain degrees, but whatever members of a congregation who have a particular calling and ability to perform the service or mission needed in the life and mission of that witnessing community. Some new models that might be explored are that of *advocate, mother,* and *layperson.*

In a church that is open for the world, *advocates* would be those with special abilities to help in bringing signs of liberation and blessing into a particular situation or need. Such people would need to have special training in their area of competence, as well as a grounding in theology as a basis for carrying out the praxis of freedom as advocates. One example of this role is that of social scientists aiding in the process of conscientization among Latin-American groups. These people are called *militant observers, coordinators,* or *animators*. They are not neutral gatherers of data. Rather they live and work with the people, gathering "the unorganized elements which already exist in the group and giving them back in organized form" in order to help clarify the direction of the liberation struggle.[66]

In a church that is open for others, another model might be that of *mother,* or nurturer.[67] This role would be quite different from the accustomed dominant position of the *Father* in church life. The minister today who is genuinely seeking to nurture a congregation to its highest potential of growth is already exercising an enabling function that is related to the cultural role usually associated with women. Both *men and women* would learn to specialize in this nurturing, enabling, and mediating role as they seek to equip others of service and dialogical action in the world.

A third model of ministry, for a church open to the future, would be that of riotous pluralism. Here the role model would be that of the *layperson,* not in the old sense of laity conceived as "domesticated clergy," but quite the reverse. Those who wish to serve in a variety of roles, using their gifts in many ways, could look to models of laypersons who have accomplished this feat even against the heavy odds of the existing clergy line. The key to independence and flexibility would be self-support. Such economic independence, already possessed by laypersons, could open the way to large numbers of people who would be free to subvert the heretical structures of the church into new forms of open ecclesiology. It would also open the way to the inclusion of all groups, men and women alike, in the direction and service of the church.

Ann Kelly and Anne Walsh have pointed out that, if we want to change the Church-clerical caste system, women will have to think of themselves as models for the future, and go beyond what is the most obvious present sign of equality in the Church, that is, ordination as we know it. Models they may find will probably also recall the origins of Christian ministry, and will point to better ways of ministering for both women and men.[68]

Whatever models may develop as we move toward the future, they will need to follow the life-style of the Representative of new humanity in such a way that openness for service will lead to a continuing process of communion and dialogue as the praxis of freedom. Only then will we be moving in the direction of a vocation for every Christian that is one of both action on behalf of others, and reflection on the meaning of Tradition for their own lives and actions of liberation in society.

PROLOGUE

We have only just begun the search for human liberation in a feminist perspective. No one knows what it would be like "if they gave a revolution and everybody won." No one knows how it would be to live in a truly androgynous world where men and women were equal and each one could express his or her life-style in a variety of ways. No one knows how the oppressed peoples of the world can move together to eliminate barriers of sex, race, and class which deprive human beings of the praxis of freedom. And no one knows the variety of ways in which the renewal of the church for mission might take place. In this light, it is fitting to end with a *prologue* or invitation to each person and group to join the others who have begun, in a continuing experiment of humanization.

For Christians, this experiment in liberation is not done only on our own initiative. It is a way of participating in the humanity of God; joining God's experiment in being together with us, so that we might be together in community with each other. We are not without clues in this divine-human experiment, for we already know the meaning of true humanity in the Second Adam who represents the beginning of that humanity and the living and still-evolving memory of our future with God and with one another. In the short range, we have the day-to-day signs of *shalom* and wholeness which we experience as gifts in the midst of life. In the long

, we have the expectation of the full restoration of the ₀.ᵤₐning universe, waiting on tiptoe for the revealing of the children of God (Rom. 8:19).

This book itself is an experiment in liberation theology— an invitation to test out the signs of the times in the light of Tradition, so that we can begin to speak the language of hope in a world where there is little hope. It is an experiment, not just because this is where we are in the search for human liberation, but because this is always the nature of liberation theology. The method of this type of theology is that of asking questions and exploring possible alternatives through action-reflection. In this sense, every exercise in theological praxis is a new beginning in a continuing process and never a conclusion.

Perhaps it would help each of us to continue with our new beginnings if we were to analyze the way that liberation theology is an *experiment* in a historical and changing world. The Latin word from which the English word "experiment" is derived is *experiri* (probe, test, try). It is related to the word *periculum*, or peril. The root of the word, *per*, points us to three important dimensions of what we are trying to do in the praxis of liberation theology: *probe, experience,* and *peril.*

To *probe* is a traditional aspect of the science of theology. In the first five centuries the church considered God to be so much of a mystery that one could not "probe" directly. What people could do was to test or try out the meaning of the *oikonomia* of God's "house-holding" as revealed in the world and Christ. Later, Western theology began to investigate God, not only as a mystery but also as a problem. Usually the method of probing was that of *metaphysics* in which answers were sought in natural as well as in revealed theology. Today liberation theology carries on its testing primarily in the area of *metachronics:* looking for signals of the coming liberation of God's future in the Biblical witness and in the events of the world. It seeks to speak of the things that are unseen, because it trusts the words of promise which it hears. It continues to probe because this Word moves from hope to new hope against anything that may contradict it.

The things hoped for are not simply future events. They shape us, touch us, and hurt us *now.* Liberation theology is also rooted in *experience:* the act of trying things out by "putting our bodies on the line" (cf. Rom. 12:1). This praxis model helps us to proclaim the coming of God's liberation and blessing into the world now, and to celebrate the presence of new humanity in our midst.

Such a praxis is always one fraught with *peril* or risk. There is the constant possibility of being let down, being defeated in our actions and put to shame in our hope. The promise of God is not a guarantee *(securitas).* It offers certainty *(certitudo)* in God's humanity, but not security in which we have all the answers. God is faithful to the promise, but this does not mean that the way will be easy for anyone who seeks to become a representative of new humanity. The image for our action is always that of the *'ebed Yahweh,* the suffering servant. The way of experiment leads through the cross as we seek to become servants for Christ's sake. In the midst of this peril, liberation theology must always be ready to give the *logos* of its hope, working to relate action and reflection in a discipline of praxis.

This is what we have been about in these pages: relating the experience of both oppression and liberation to the Tradition of Jesus Christ. In its presentation of liberation theology, the book is a sign of liberation now! It is *now* that "the time has come for judgment to begin with the household of God" (I Peter 4:17). It is *now* that liberation and new humanity have begun. It is *now* that we must risk the praxis of freedom so that God's will is done on *earth* as it is in heaven!

NOTES

Introduction

1. B. Friedan, J. Reinach, J. Rene, *Liberation Now* (Claro Corporation, Decca, 32728).

2. Raden Adjeng Kartini, cited by Bernhard Dahm, *History of Indonesia in the Twentieth Century* (Praeger Publishers, 1971), p. 21.

3. Martin Marty, *The Search for a Usable Future* (Harper & Row, Publishers, Inc., 1969), p. 12.

4. Tish Sommers, *The Not-So-Helpless Female* (David McKay Company, Inc., 1973), pp. 231–232.

5. Mary Daly, *The Church and the Second Sex* (Harper & Row, Publishers, Inc., 1968), pp. 147–148.

6. Some of the more recent books on liberation theology are: Rubem Alves, *A Theology of Human Hope* (Corpus Books, 1969); James Cone, *A Black Theology of Liberation* (J. B. Lippincott Company, 1970); Gustavo Gutiérrez, *A Theology of Liberation*, tr. and ed. by Caridad Inda and John Eagleson (Orbis Books, 1972); Frederick Herzog, *Liberation Theology* (The Seabury Press, Inc., 1972); J. Deotis Roberts, *Liberation and Reconciliation: A Black Theology* (The Westminster Press, 1971); Rosemary Radford Ruether, *Liberation Theology* (Paulist Press, 1973); Letty M. Russell, *Ferment of Freedom* (National Board, YWCA, 1972); Mary Daly, *Beyond God the Father: Toward a Philosophy of Women's Liberation* (Beacon Press, Inc., 1973). The author indicates that her book is on philosophy and not to be identified with "patriarchal

religion," p. 6. William R. Jones, *Is God a White Racist? A Preamble to Black Theology* (Doubleday & Company, Inc., Anchor Book, 1973). The author presents a critique of black liberation theology on the basis of its inability to account for black suffering.

7. Gutiérrez, *Theology of Liberation*, p. 307; cf. Cone, *Black Theology*, p. 17.

8. Jürgen Moltmann, *Theology of Hope*, tr. by James W. Leitch (Harper & Row, Publishers, Inc., 1967); Jürgen Moltmann, *Religion, Revolution and the Future* (Charles Scribner's Sons, 1969); Johannes Metz, *Theology of the World* (Herder & Herder, Inc., 1969).

9. Jürgen Moltmann, "Political Theology," *Theology Today*, April, 1971, pp. 8, 23; cf. Johannes Metz, "Political Theology," in Karl Rahner and others (eds.), *Sacramentum Mundi* (Herder & Herder, Inc., 1970), Vol. V, pp. 34–38.

10. Barbara Burris, "The Fourth World Manifesto," in Anne Koedt and Shulamith Firestone (eds.), *Notes from the Third Year: Women's Liberation* (P.O. Box AA, Old Chelsea Station, New York, N.Y. 10011, 1972), p. 118.

1: JOURNEY TOWARD FREEDOM

1. Marlene Dixon, "Why Women's Liberation?" in Elsie Adams and Mary Louise Briscoe (eds.), *Up Against the Wall, Mother* (The Free Press, 1971), pp. 419–433.

2. Pauli Murray, "Racism and Sexism: The Liberation of Black Women," in Mary Lou Thompson (ed.), *Voices of New Feminism* (Beacon Press, Inc., 1970), pp. 82–102.

3. Moltmann, *Theology*, p. 105.

4. Billy Taylor and Dick Douglas, "I Wish I Knew How It Would Feel to Be Free" (Duane Music, Inc., 565 Fifth Avenue, New York, N.Y. 10017, 1964 el1968).

5. Unless otherwise indicated, all Bible quotations are from the *Revised Standard Version of the Holy Bible* (Thomas Nelson & Sons, 1952, 1946). Translations in this chapter are a free paraphrase by the author in consultation with Hans Hoekendijk, unless otherwise indicated; cf. Hans

Hoekendijk, "Bible Study on Romans 8:13–27," *Concept* (Geneva: World Council of Churches, DSME/M 69:25), pp. 20–25.

6. Rubem Alves, *Tomorrow's Child* (Harper & Row, Publishers, Inc., 1972), p. 191.

7. Moltmann, *Religion,* pp. 66–67.

8. Lucinda Cisler, "Women: A Bibliography," in Thompson (ed.), *Voices,* pp. 217–246; *Women* (Packet of materials from women on six continents, P.O. Box 187, Dayton View Station, Dayton, Ohio 44206).

9. Juliet Mitchell, "The Longest Revolution," in Betty Roszak and Theodore Roszak (eds.), *Masculine/Feminine: Readings in Sexual Mythology and Liberation of Women* (Harper & Row, Publishers, Inc., 1969), pp. 161–164.

10. August Bebel, *Woman Under Socialism* (first published in 1883; Shocken Books, Inc., 1971), p. 9. Cf. Shulamith Firestone, *The Dialectic of Sex: The Case for Feminist Revolution* (Bantam Books, Inc., 1970), pp. 1–14.

11. "Report of the National Conference on the Role of Women in Theological Education," in Sally Bentley Doely (ed.), *Women's Liberation and the Church* (Association Press, 1971), Appendix, p. 136.

12. Moltmann, *Religion,* p. 77.

13. Joseph Comblin, "Le Thème de la liberation dans la pensée chrétienne latino-américaine," *La Revue Nouvelle* (Brussels), May–June 1972, pp. 560–574. English translation in *LADOC* (Latin American Documentation Center, Washington, D.C.), No. 30 (Sept. 1972), pp. 5–7.

14. Gutiérrez, *Theology of Liberation,* p. xi.

15. Hans Hoekendijk, *Horizons of Hope* (Tidings, 1970), pp. 32–33.

16. Paulo Freire, *Pedagogy of the Oppressed* (Herder & Herder, Inc., 1970), p. 159.

17. H. Hoekendijk, *Horizons,* p. 32.

18. Moltmann, *Religion,* pp. 50–51; Ernst Käsemann, *Jesus Means Freedom* (Fortress Press, 1969), p. 73.

19. Käsemann, *Jesus Means Freedom,* p. 39.

20. *Ibid.,* p. 83.

21. Dorothy Sayre, *Are Women Human?* (Wm. B. Eerd-

mans Publishing Company, 1971), p. 47.

22. Paulo Freire, *Education for Critical Awareness* (The Seabury Press, Inc., 1973), pp. 46–47.

23. Max Weber, "Class, Status, Party," in C. Wright Mills (ed.), *Images of Man* (George Braziller, Inc., 1960), pp. 121–135; cf. Firestone, *Dialectic of Sex*, p. 2.

24. Valerie Russell, "Racism and Sexism: A Collective Struggle," *The Woman Packet* (Church Women United, Box 134, Manhattanville Station, New York, N.Y. 10027, 1972).

25. Doris Wright, "On Black Womanhood," *The Woman Packet* (1972); Frances M. Beal, "Double Jeopardy: To Be Black and Female," in Robin Morgan (ed.), *Sisterhood Is Powerful* (Random House, Inc., Vintage Books, 1970), pp. 340–359.

26. Shirley Chisholm, "Women Must Rebel," in Thompson (ed.), *Voices*, p. 216.

27. Letty M. Russell, "Rapidation in the Church," *Risk*, V:3/4 (1969), pp. 58–67.

28. Moltmann, *Theology*, p. 310.

29. Julius Lester, Unpublished speech at the conference on "Chaos Invading Cosmos—A Reshaping of Hope" (University of Kansas, 1973).

30. Moltmann, *Theology*, p. 20.

31. Ferdinand Kerstiens, "Hope," *Sacramentum Mundi* (Herder & Herder, Inc., 1969), Vol. III, p. 65.

32. Jürgen Moltmann, Unpublished speech at the Duke University Conference on Hope, 1968 (mimeographed notes of Thomas Herrin), p. 20.

33. Alves, *Theology*, p. 118.

34. Jürgen Moltmann, "Antwort auf die Kritik der Theologie der Hoffnung," in Wolf-Dieter Marsch (ed.), *Diskussion über die "Theologie der Hoffnung"* (Munich: Chr. Kaiser Verlag, 1967), pp. 201–215.

35. Alves, *Tomorrow's Child*, p. 191.

36. Dana Densmore, "On Sisterhood," in Adams and Briscoe (eds.), *Up Against the Wall, Mother*, p. 475.

37. Marge Wold, "A Paradigm of Liberation" (Unpublished speech to the South Pacific District Convention, American Lutheran Church, May 3–6, 1963); *Women Exploring Theol-*

ogy at Grailville, 1972 (Church Women United, New York, N.Y. 10027).

38. William F. Arndt and F. Wilbur Gingrich (eds.), *A Greek-English Lexicon of the New Testament* (The University of Chicago Press, 1957), p. 715.

39. Alves, *Theology,* p. 105.

2: HUMAN LIBERATION AND THEOLOGY

1. Gutiérrez, *Theology of Liberation,* p. 145.

2. Marty, *The Search for a Usable Future,* pp. 78–79.

3. Harvey Cox, "Eight Theses on Female Liberation," *Christianity and Crisis,* XXXI:16 (Oct. 4, 1971), pp. 199–202; Leonard Swidler, "Jesus Was a Feminist," *Catholic World,* January, 1971, pp. 177–184; Anonymous article from South Africa, "Towards a Theology of Sexual Politics" (mimeographed); Eric Mount, Jr., *The Feminine Factor* (John Knox Press, 1973).

4. John A. T. Robinson, *The New Reformation?* (The Westminster Press, 1965), pp. 60–61.

5. Ruether, *Liberation,* p. 2.

6. J. C. Hoekendijk, *The Church Inside Out* (The Westminster Press, 1966), p. 79; Thomas Aquinas, "Scientia Conclusionum," *Religion in Geschichte und Gegenwart* (3d ed., 1962), Vol. VI, p. 777.

7. Ruether, *Liberation,* p. 3; cf. also Sheila Collins, "Toward a Feminist Theology," *The Christian Century,* Aug. 2, 1972, pp. 796, 799; Mary Daly, "Post-Christian Theology: Some Connections Between Idolatry and Methodolatry, Between Deicide and Methodicide," *Women and Religion, 1973 Proceedings,* comp. by Joan Arnold Romero (American Academy of Religion, Florida State University, Tallahassee, Florida, 1973).

8. Alves, *Tomorrow's Child,* p. 182; cf. Cone, *Black Theology,* pp. 30–34.

9. Freire, *Pedagogy,* p. 75; cf. Rosiska Darcy de Oliveria and Mireille Calame, "Liberation of Woman: To Change the World and Re-invent Life," *IDAC 3* (1973) (Institute of Cul-

tural Action, 27, chemin de Crêts, 1218 Grand Saconney, Geneva, Switzerland).

10. Alves, *Tomorrow's Child*, pp. 182–205.

11. Gutiérrez, *Theology of Liberation*, p. 308; Herzog, *Liberation Theology*, p. 16.

12. Ferdinand Hahn, *Mission in the New Testament* (Alec R. Allenson, Inc., 1965), pp. 18–19.

13. Comblin, "Le Thème de la liberation," *La Revue Nouvelle*, May–June 1972, pp. 8–9.

14. Moltmann, *Religion*, p. 81.

15. Käsemann, *Jesus Means Freedom*, p. 9; Cone, *Black Theology*, pp. 19–22.

16. Daly, *Beyond*, p. 28.

17. Letty M. Russell, "Women's Liberation in a Biblical Perspective," *Concern*, XIII:5 (May–June 1971).

18. Alves, *Theology*, "The Historicity of Freedom," pp. 85–100.

19. Gutiérrez, *Theology of Liberation*, pp. 1–10; Gerhard von Rad, *The Theology of Israel's Prophetic Tradition*, Vol. II of *Old Testament Theology* (Harper & Row, Publishers, Inc., 1965), pp. 101–106.

20. Gerhard Ebeling, *Word and Faith* (Fortress Press, 1963), pp. 364–373, Ch. XIV, "The World as History."

21. Jürgen Moltmann, *Hope and Planning* (Harper & Row, Publishers, Inc., 1961), pp. 178–184; "The Christian Theology of Hope and Its Bearing on Development," in *In Search of a Theology of Development* (Geneva: SODEPAX, 1970), pp. 93–100.

22. Dorothee Sölle, "The Gospel and Liberation," *Commonweal*, Dec. 22, 1972, p. 270; cf. Dorothee Sölle, *Political Theology* (Fortress Press, 1974).

23. Freire, *Pedagogy*, p. 72.

24. Comblin, "Le Thème de la liberation," *La Revue Nouvelle*, May–June 1972, p. 8; Herzog, *Liberation Theology*, p. 261.

25. Werner Post, "Ideology," *Sacramentum Mundi*, Vol. III, pp. 94–97; Oliveria and Calame, "Liberation of Woman," *IDAC 3*, pp. 10–16.

26. H. Hoekendijk, *Horizons*, pp. 32–33.

27. "Detroit 1969," in Doely (ed.), *Women's Liberation and the Church*, Appendix I, pp. 97–100; cf. "Women in Church and Society," *Asia Focus*, VII:3 (East Asia Christian Conference, 1972), p. 3.

28. "Pastoral Constitution on the Church in the Modern World," in Walter M. Abbott (ed.), *The Documents of Vatican II* (Guild Press, Ltd., 1966), p. 224, par. 25; Herzog, *Liberation Theology*, p. 15.

29. H. Richard Niebuhr, *Christ and Culture* (Harper Torchbook, 1956), p. 195; Hans Hoekendijk, "Working Paper for the WCC Study of the Role of Christians Within Changing Institutions" (mimeographed, Fall 1971), p. 23.

30. James Cone, "Black Theology and Reconciliation," *Christianity and Crisis*, XXXII:24 (Jan. 22, 1973), p. 307.

31. Sölle, "The Gospel and Liberation," *Commonweal*, Dec. 22, 1972, p. 273.

32. Ruether, *Liberation*, p. 124.

33. Abbott (ed.), *Documents of Vatican II*, pp. 227–228, par. 29.

34. Freire, *Pedagogy*, pp. 90–91.

35. Nelle Morton, "The Rising Woman Consciousness in a Male Language Structure," *Andover Newton Quarterly*, XII:4 (March 1972), p. 181; cf. also Alicia Craig Faxon, *Women and Jesus* (United Church Press, 1973).

36. Gutiérrez, *Theology of Liberation*, p. 146; cf. also Abbott (ed.), *Documents of Vatican II*, p. 261, par. 55.

37. Freire, *Pedagogy*, p. 19.

38. Ruether, *Liberation*, p. 13.

39. Freire, *Pedagogy*, p. 19; cf. also Russell, *Ferment*, pp. 21–28.

40. Freire, *Pedagogy*, pp. 76, 42.

41. Rosemary Ruether, "Women's Liberation in Historical and Theological Perspective," in Doely (ed.), *Women's Liberation*, pp. 31–34.

42. Mary Daly, "The Courage to See: Religious Implications of the New Sisterhood," *The Christian Century*, Sept. 22, 1971, p. 1109.

43. Cone, "Black Theology and Reconciliation," *Christianity and Crisis*, Jan. 22, 1973, p. 307; cf. also William Jones,

"Toward an Interim Assessment of Black Theology," *Reflection* (Yale Divinity School), Jan., 1972.

3: SEARCH FOR A USABLE PAST

1. Henry S. Commager, "The Search for a Usable Past," *American Heritage*, XVI:2 (Feb. 1965); cited by Marty, *The Search for a Usable Future*, p. 12.

2. Immanuel Kant, *Critique of Pure Reason* (London: J. M. Dent & Sons, Ltd., 1934), p. 457.

3. Paul S. Minear (ed.), *Faith and Order Findings* (London: SCM Press, Ltd., 1963), pp. 1–63.

4. *Ibid.*, pp. 16–18. The distinction between tradition, traditions, and Tradition is followed in this text.

5. Yves Congar, *Tradition and Traditions* (London: Burns & Oates, Ltd., 1966), pp. 135–136; Max Thurian, "Renewal and the Scripture-Tradition Problem in Light of Vatican II and Montreal 1963," in L. K. Shook (ed.), *Theology of Renewal* (Herder & Herder, Inc., 1968), Vol. I, p. 71.

6. Gerhard Ebeling, *The Problem of Historicity* (Fortress Press, 1967), pp. 37–45.

7. Letty M. Russell, "Tradition as Mission: Study of a New Current in Theology and Its Implications for Theological Education" (Unpublished doctoral thesis, Union Theological Seminary, New York, 1969); "Tradition as Mission," *Study Encounter*, VI:2 (1970), pp. 1–63.

8. Minear (ed.), *Faith and Order Findings*, pp. 18–19.

9. Peter Lengsfeld, *Überlieferung* (Paderborn: Bonifacius-Druckerei, 1960), p. 28.

10. Oscar Cullmann, "The Tradition," in *The Early Church*, ed. by A. J. B. Higgins (The Westminster Press, 1956), pp. 60, 70–72.

11. Marga Bührig, "Discrimination Against Women," in Ronald Preston (ed.), *Technology and Social Justice* (Judson Press, 1971), p. 319.

12. Josef Rupert Geiselmann, *The Meaning of Tradition* (Herder & Herder, Inc., 1966), p. 23.

13. C. Ellis Nelson, *Where Faith Begins* (John Knox Press, 1967), pp. 58–65.

14. Freire, *Pedagogy*, p. 83.

15. William Clebsch in *Criterion* (University of Chicago, Spring, 1972), cited by Anne McGrew Bennett, "Women in the New Society," *Journal of Current Social Issues*, II:1 (Winter 1972–1973), p. 25; Firestone, *Dialectic of Sex*, pp. 15–40.

16. James Cone, *The Spirituals and the Blues: An Interpretation* (The Seabury Press, Inc., 1972); cf. Gerda Lerner (ed.), *Black Women in White America: A Documentary History* (Pantheon Books, 1972).

17. Florence Howe, "No Ivory Towers Need Apply," *Ms.*, II:3 (Sept. 1973), p. 78; cf. Gerda Lerner, *The Grimke Sisters from North Carolina: Rebels Against Slavery* (Houghton Mifflin Company, 1967).

18. Ebeling, *Word*, pp. 363–364.

19. *Ibid.*, pp. 362, 364; cf. Gordon D. Kaufman, "The Imago Dei as Man's Historicity," *The Journal of Religion*, XXXVI:3 (July 1956), pp. 157–168.

20. Moltmann, *Religion*, p. 51; cf. William Hordern, *Introduction* (Vol. I of *New Directions in Theology Today*, 7 vols.; The Westminster Press, 1966), pp. 66–73; Carl E. Braaten, *History and Hermeneutics* (Vol. II of *New Directions;* 1966), pp. 60–61.

21. Moltmann, *Theology*, pp. 77, 230–272.

22. Samuel Terrien, "Toward a Biblical Theology of Womanhood," *Religion in Life*, Autumn 1973, pp. 322–333.

23. Bennett, "Women in the New Society," *Journal of Current Social Issues*, Winter 1972–1973, p. 27; Terrien, "Toward a Biblical Theology of Womanhood," *Religion in Life*, Autumn 1973, p. 326.

24. Terrien, "Toward a Biblical Theology of Womanhood," *Religion in Life*, Autumn 1973, p. 329.

25. Terrien, *ibid.*, p. 330; Krister Stendahl, *The Bible and the Role of Women* (Fortress Press, 1966), pp. 25–37; Faxon, *Women and Jesus*.

26. Letty M. Russell, "Christianity," *According to the Scriptures: The Image of Woman Portrayed in the Sacred Writings of the World's Major Religions* (Geneva: World Young Women's Christian Association, 1972), pp. 10–14; Ferdinand Hahn, *The Worship of the Early Church* (Fortress Press, 1973), pp. 74–75.

27. Elaine H. Pagels, *The Johannine Gospel in Gnostic*

Exegesis (Abingdon Press, 1973); André Dumas, "Biblical Anthropology and the Participation of Women in the Ministry of the Church," *Concerning the Ordination of Women* (Geneva: World Council of Churches, 1964), p. 28.

28. Joan Morris, *The Lady Was a Bishop* (The Macmillan Company, 1973); Roland Bainton, *Women of the Reformation*, 2 vols. (Augsburg Publishing House, 1971, 1973); R. Pierce Beaver, *All Loves Excelling: American Protestant Women in World Mission* (Wm. B. Eerdmans Publishing Company, 1968).

29. W. H. C. Frend, *The Donatist Church: A Movement of Protest in Roman Africa* (Oxford: Clarendon Press, 1952); A. H. M. Jones, *Were Ancient Heresies Disguised Social Movements?* (Fortress Press, 1966).

30. Bengt G. M. Sundkler, *Bantu Prophets in South Africa* (London: Lutterworth Press, 1968); G. C. Ousthuizen, *Post-Christianity in Africa* (Wm. B. Eerdmans Publishing Company, 1968).

31. Mircea Eliade, *Myth and Reality* (Harper Torchbook, 1963), p. 5.

32. Thomas O'Dea, *The Sociology of Religion* (Prentice-Hall, Inc., 1966), pp. 41–42; G. Van der Leeuw, *Religion in Essence and Manifestation* (Harper Torchbook, 1963), Vol. II, pp. 413–415.

33. Karl Marx, *Writings of the Young Marx on Philosophy and Society*, tr. and ed. by Lloyd D. Easton and Kurt H. Guddat (Doubleday & Company, Inc., Anchor Book, 1967), p. 402; O'Dea, *Sociology of Religion*, p. 64.

34. Braaten, *History and Hermeneutics*, pp. 33–52.

35. Gerhard von Rad, *The Theology of Israel's Historical Traditions*, Vol. I of *Old Testament Theology* (Harper & Row, Publishers, Inc., 1962), pp. 136–139; Terrien, "Toward a Biblical Theology of Womanhood," *Religion in Life*, Autumn 1973, p. 324; Mircea Eliade, *The Sacred and the Profane* (Harcourt, Brace and Company, Inc., 1959), pp. 95–113.

36. Von Rad, *Old Testament Theology*, Vol. I, pp. 136–139.

37. Theodor Reik, *The Creation of Woman* (McGraw-Hill Book Co., Inc., 1960), pp. 126–132; *Women Exploring Theology at Grailville*, 1972; Lilly Rivlin, "Lilith," *Ms.*, I:6 (Dec. 1972), pp. 92–97, 114–115.

38. Terrien, "Toward a Biblical Theology of Womanhood," *Religion in Life,* Autumn 1973, pp. 324–327; Phyllis Trible, "Eve and Adam: Genesis 2–3 Reread," *Andover Newton Quarterly,* XIII:4 (March 1973), pp. 251–257; Walter Brueggemann, "Of the Same Flesh and Bone (Genesis 2:23a)," *The Catholic Biblical Quarterly,* XXXII (1970), pp. 532–543.

39. Freire, *Pedagogy,* pp. 135–136.

40. Freire, *Education,* p. xi.

41. Warren Farrell, "Resocializing Men's Attitudes: Toward Women's Role in Society" (Paper read at the American Political Science Association Annual Convention, Los Angeles, Sept. 9, 1970), pp. 6–9 (mimeographed).

42. Simone de Beauvoir, *The Second Sex* (Bantam Books, Inc., 1949), pp. xvi *et passim.*

43. Mary Daly, "The Spiritual Revolution: Women's Liberation as Theological Re-education," *Andover Newton Quarterly,* XII:4 (March 1972), p. 169.

44. Harvey Cox, *The Seduction of the Spirit* (Simon & Schuster, Inc., 1973), pp. 191–193.

45. Casey Miller and Kate Swift, "Desexing Language," *Ms.,* Dec. 20, 1971, pp. 103–104; Alma Graham, "How to Make Trouble: The Making of a Nonsexist Dictionary," *Ms.,* II:6 (Dec. 1973), pp. 12–14.

46. Morton, "Rising Woman Consciousness," *Andover Newton Quarterly,* March, 1972, p. 182. Cf. Anne Patrick, "Consciousness Raising and the Liturgical Crisis," *Liturgy,* Journal of the Liturgical Conference, XVIII:10 (Dec. 1973), pp. 7–11.

47. de Beauvoir, *Second Sex,* p. xxvi.

48. Stendahl, *Bible and the Role of Women,* pp. 7–34.

49. *Ibid.,* p. 20.

50. Karl Rahner, "Divine Trinity," *Sacramentum Mundi,* Vol. VI, p. 302.

51. Dumas, "Biblical Anthropology," in *Concerning the Ordination of Women,* p. 24.

52. Moltmann, *Religion,* pp. 208–212.

53. *Ibid.,* p. 209.

54. Von Rad, *Old Testament Theology,* Vol. I, pp. 181–182.

55. *Ibid.*

56. B. W. Anderson, "God, Names of," *The Interpreter's*

Dictionary of the Bible, 4 vols. (Abingdon Press, 1962), Vol. II, p. 410; Stephen Verney, *People and Cities* (Fleming H. Revell Company, 1969), p. 110.

57. Martin Noth, *Exodus, A Commentary* (The Westminster Press, 1962), p. 43.

58. Von Rad, *Old Testament Theology*, Vol. I, pp. 180, 185; Gutiérrez, *Theology of Liberation*, p. 165.

59. Robert H. Pfeiffer, *Introduction to the Old Testament* (Harper & Brothers, 1941), pp. 74 ff.; W. D. Davies, *Invitation to the New Testament* (Doubleday & Company, Inc., 1968), p. 27. Cited by Bennett, "Women in the New Society," *Journal of Current Social Issues*, Winter 1972–1973, p. 27, fn. 37.

60. Von Rad, *Old Testament Theology*, Vol. I, p. 181; Brueggemann, "Of the Same Flesh," *The Catholic Biblical Quarterly*, 1970, p. 539.

61. Von Rad, *Old Testament Theology*, Vol. I, p. 145.

62. Bennett, "Women in the New Society," *Journal of Current Social Issues*, Winter 1972–1973; J. Edgar Bruns, *God as Woman, Woman as God* (Paulist Press, 1973), pp. 35–36.

63. Von Rad, *Old Testament Theology*, Vol. I, pp. 146–147; Kaufman, "The Imago Dei as Man's Historicity," *The Journal of Religion*, July 1956, pp. 162–165.

64. Von Rad, *Old Testament Theology*, Vol. I, p. 150; Clarence Vos, *Woman in Old Testament Worship* (Published dissertation, Amsterdam, Free University, 1968), p. 19.

65. Terrien, "Toward a Biblical Theology of Womanhood," *Religion in Life*, Autumn 1973, p. 324; cf. Trible, "Eve and Adam," *Andover Newton Quarterly*, March 1973, p. 252; Dumas, "Biblical Anthropology," in *Concerning the Ordination of Women*, p. 30; Brueggemann, "Of the Same Flesh," *The Catholic Biblical Quarterly*, 1970, pp. 541–542.

66. John A. T. Robinson, *Honest to God* (The Westminster Press, 1963), pp. 74–75.

67. P. Gerlach, "Henne," *Lexikon der christlichen Ikonographie*, 4 vols. (Verlag Herder, 1970), Vol. II, pp. 241 ff.; W. S. McCullough, "Hen," *Interpreter's Dictionary*, Vol. II, p. 581; J. Hempel, *Gott und Mensch im Alten Testament* (Stuttgart: W. Kohlhammer, 1936), pp. 141–142.

68. J. A. Wharton, "Wing," *Interpreter's Dictionary*, Vol. IV, p. 852.

69. Terrien, "Toward a Biblical Theology of Womanhood," *Religion in Life*, Autumn 1973, p. 328.

70. Dumas, "Biblical Anthropology," in *Concerning the Ordination of Women*, p. 23.

71. Bennett, "Women in the New Society," *Journal of Current Social Issues*, Winter 1972–1973; Penelope Washburn Chen, "Rediscovering the Feminine in God," *The Tower* (Union Theological Seminary, New York), XVII:3 (Spring 1971), pp. 9, 12; Bruns, *God as Woman*, pp. 36–40.

72. W. D. Davies, *Paul and Rabbinic Judaism* (London: S.P.C.K., 1955), p. 150.

73. *Ibid.*, p. 154.

74. S. V. McCasland, "Spirit," *Interpreter's Dictionary*, Vol. IV, pp. 432–434; Bruns, *God as Woman*, pp. 39–40.

75. Dumas, "Biblical Anthropology," *Concerning the Ordination of Women*, p. 24; Bruns, *God as Woman*, p. 40.

76. Ann Belford Ulanov, *The Feminine in Jungian Psychology and in Christian Theology* (Northwestern University Press, 1971), p. 308.

77. James Cone, "The Dialectic of Theology and Life" (Inaugural lecture as professor of theology, Union Theological Seminary, New York City, Oct. 11, 1973).

78. Terrien, "Toward a Biblical Theology of Womanhood," *Religion in Life*, Autumn 1973, p. 333.

4: Salvation and Conscientization

1. J. Verkuyl, *The Message of Liberation in Our Age* (Wm. B. Eerdmans Publishing Company, 1970), pp. 16–17.

2. Gutiérrez, *Theology of Liberation*, p. 149.

3. Verkuyl, *Message*, p. 12.

4. *Bangkok Assembly 1973: Minutes and Report of the Assembly of the Commission on World Mission and Evangelism* (Geneva: World Council of Churches, 1973), pp. 1–2.

5. *Ibid.*, p. 1; Verkuyl, *Message*, p. 14; Emilio Castro,

"Bangkok, the New Opportunity," *International Review of Mission*, LXII (April 1973), pp. 138–139.

6. M. M. Thomas, "The Meaning of Salvation Today—A Personal Statement," *IRM*, April, 1973, p. 165; Jürgen Moltmann, *The Gospel of Liberation* (Word, Inc., 1973), pp. 88–89.

7. Verkuyl, *Message*, pp. 26–27.

8. Donald McGavran (ed.), *Eye of the Storm: The Great Debate in Mission* (Word Books, 1971); Ralph Winter (ed.), *The Evangelical Response to Bangkok* (Pasadena: William Carey Library, 1973).

9. Verkuyl, *Message*, pp. 17–21; Alan Richardson, "Salvation, Savior," *Interpreter's Dictionary*, Vol. IV, p. 169; W. Eisenbein, *Die Wurzel sh-l-m im Alten Testament (Beiträge zur Alttestamentlichen Wissenschaft*, 1969); L. Rost, "Erwägungen zum Begriff sh-l-m," in K. H. Bernhardt (ed.), *Schalom* (1971).

10. Johannes Pedersen, *Israel: Its Life and Culture*, 4 vols. (London: Oxford University Press, 1954), I–II, p. 330; John I. Durham, "Shalom and the Presence of God," in John I. Durham and J. R. Porter (eds.), *Proclamation and Presence* (London: SCM Press, Ltd., 1970), pp. 275–292.

11. Claus Westermann, "Der Friede (schalom) im Alten Testament," *Zeichen der Zeit*, X (1970), pp. 361–375; Claus Westermann, *Theologie: 6 × 12 Hauptbegriffe* (Stuttgart: Kreuz-Verlag, 1967), "Rettung oder Heil," pp. 13–17; "Segen," pp. 17–20; "Frieden," pp. 58–63; Verkuyl, *Message*, p. 18.

12. W. J. Harrelson, "Blessings and Cursings," *Interpreter's Dictionary*, Vol. I, pp. 446–448; Gerhard Wehmeier, *Der Segen im Alten Testament* (Basel: Reinhardt, 1970).

13. Pedersen, *Israel*, I–II, pp. 182, 190, 212; Claus Westermann, *Der Segen in der Bibel und im Handeln der Kirche* (Munich: Chr. Kaiser-Verlag, 1968).

14. A. Richardson, "Salvation, Savior," *Interpreter's Dictionary*, Vol. IV, pp. 177–181; W. Foerster, "Sotēria," in Gerhard Kittel and Gerhard Friedrich (eds.), *Theological Dictionary of the New Testament*, 9 vols. (Wm. B. Eerdmans Publishing Co., 1964–1974).

15. "Extra Ecclesiam Nulla Salus," Karl Rahner and Herbert Vorgrimler, *Theological Dictionary* (Herder & Herder, Inc., 1965), pp. 162–163.

16. Piet Schoonenberg, "Sin," *Sacramentum Mundi*, Vol. VI, pp. 87–92.

17. S. J. De Vries, "Sin, Sinners," *Interpreter's Dictionary*, Vol. IV, p. 361.

18. *Ibid.*, p. 373.

19. Gutiérrez, *Theology of Liberation*, p. 150.

20. *Salvation Today and Contemporary Experience: A Collection of Texts for Critical Study and Reflection* (Geneva: World Council of Churches, 1972).

21. Gabriel Fackre, *Do and Tell: Engagement Evangelism in the '70s* (Wm. B. Eerdmans Publishing Company, 1973), p. 34; Letty M. Russell, "Shalom in Postmodern Society," in John A. Westerhoff III (ed.), *A Colloquy on Christian Education* (United Church Press, 1972), pp. 97–105; *Colloquy*, National Shalom Conference Issue, VI:3 (March 1973).

22. Fackre, *Do and Tell*, p. 86; *Colloquy, A Curriculum for Peace*, 5:7 (July/August 1972).

23. Gutiérrez, *Theology of Liberation*, p. 151; cf. A. Schoors, *I Am God Your Savior* (Leiden: E. J. Brill, 1973).

24. Cone, "Dialectic of Theology and Life"; cf. "Black Theology and Reconciliation," *Christianity and Crisis*, Jan. 22, 1973, pp. 303–308.

25. René Laurentin, *Liberation, Development and Salvation* (Orbis Books, 1972), p. 53.

26. Ruether, *Liberation*, pp. 7–9, 16–22; Sölle, "The Gospel and Liberation," *Commonweal*, Dec. 22, 1972, p. 270.

27. Sölle, "The Gospel and Liberation," *Commonweal*, Dec. 22, 1972, pp. 273–274; cf. Kaufman, "Imago Dei," *The Journal of Religion*, July, 1956, pp. 165–167.

28. A. Richardson, "Salvation, Savior," *Interpreter's Dictionary*, Vol. IV, p. 169; Verkuyl, *Message*, pp. 17–18.

29. Gutiérrez, *Theology of Liberation*, p. 175; cf. Ruether, *Liberation*, p. 8.

30. Daly, *Church and the Second Sex*, pp. 46–47; cf. Ruether, *Liberation*, "Is Christianity Misogynist?" pp. 95–113.

31. Valarie Saiving Goldstein, "The Human Situation: A Feminine View," *The Journal of Religion*, XL:2 (April 1960), pp. 108–109.

32. Oliveria and Calame, *IDAC 3*, p. 1.

33. Paulo Freire, "Conscientizing as a Way of Liberating," *LADOC*, II, p. 29a (mimeographed reprint), p. 5; Freire, *Pedagogy*, p. 157.

34. Freire, "Conscientizing," *LADOC*, p. 5; cf. Oliveria and Calame, *IDAC 3*, pp. 2–4.

35. Albert H. van den Heuvel, "Secularization as Freedom and Yoke," *The Humiliation of the Church* (The Westminster Press, 1966), pp. 11–29; Larry Shiner, *The Secularization of History, An Introduction to the Theology of Friedrich Gogarten* (Abingdon Press, 1966), *passim*.

36. Cornelis van Peursen, "Man and Reality—The History of Human Thought," *Student World* (World Student Christian Federation), LVI:1 (1963), pp. 13–21, reprinted in John Bowden and James Richmond (eds.), *A Reader in Contemporary Theology* (The Westminster Press, 1967), pp. 115–126.

37. Philip R. Phoenix, "Functional Approach to the Understanding of Ministry," *Theological Education*, IV:1 (Autumn 1967), p. 540; Karl W. Deutsch, *The Nerves of Government: Models of Political Communication and Control* (The Free Press, 1966), p. 8.

38. Freire, "Conscientizing," *LADOC*, pp. 2–3.

39. *Ibid.*

40. *Ibid.*

41. Thomas Sanders, "The Theology of Liberation: Christian Utopianism," and Rubem Alves, "Christian Realism: Ideology of the Establishment," *Christianity and Crisis*, XXXIII:15 (Sept. 17, 1973), pp. 167–176; cf. "Thomas Sanders Replies," *Christianity and Crisis*, XXXIII:20 (Nov. 26, 1973), pp. 249–251.

42. Freire, "Conscientizing," *LADOC*, p. 5.

43. Doely (ed.), *Women's Liberation*, pp. 33–36.

44. Morton, "Rising Woman Consciousness," *Andover Newton Quarterly*, March, 1972, p. 178.

45. Tish Sommers, "A Feminist Challenge to Humanism" (Paper read at the Symposium: Human Potential for Political

Change, The Association of Humanistic Psychology, June, 1973); cf. Sommers, *The Not-So-Helpless Female.*

46. R. C. and H. Thurnwald, *Black and White in East Africa* (London, 1935), p. 377; cf. Rosemary Radford Ruether, "Sexism and Theology of Liberation," *The Christian Century,* Dec. 12, 1973, pp. 1224–1229.

47. Ruether, "Women's Liberation," in Doely (ed.), *Women's Liberation,* pp. 34–35.

48. B. and T. Roszak (eds.), *Masculine/Feminine,* "The WITCH Manifesto," p. 259; "The SCUM Manifesto," p. 262; "The BITCH Manifesto," p. 275.

49. Morton, "Rising Woman Consciousness," *Andover Newton Quarterly,* March, 1972.

50. Karen Bloomquist, "Women's Rising Consciousness: Implications for the Curriculum," *Theological Education* (Women in Theological Education: Past, Present, Future), VIII:4 (Summer 1972), p. 239.

51. Ruether, "Women's Liberation," in Doely (ed.), *Women's Liberation,* p. 35.

52. Peggy Way, "An Authority of Possibility for Women in the Church," in Doely (ed.), *Women's Liberation,* p. 77; cf. John David Maguire, "The Necessity of Thinking Black" (Paper delivered at the Student YWCA, University of Illinois, May, 1970).

53. Philip Potter, "Christ's Mission and Ours in Today's World," *IRM,* LXII (April 1973), p. 151.

54. W. A. Quanbeck, "Repentance," *Interpreter's Dictionary,* Vol. IV, pp. 33–34.

55. Cox, *The Seduction of the Spirit,* p. 172.

56. Morton, "Rising Woman Consciousness," *Andover Newton Quarterly,* March, 1972, p. 179.

57. Cone, "Black Theology and Reconciliation," *Christianity and Crisis,* Jan. 22, 1973, pp. 303–308.

58. Carol Christ and Marilyn Collins, "Shattering the Idols of Men: Theology from the Perspective of Women's Experience," *Reflection* (Yale Divinity School), LXIX:4 (March 1972), p. 12; cf. Ruether, "Sexism," *The Christian Century,* Dec. 12, 1973, p. 1226.

59. Heinrich Heppe, *Reformed Dogmatics* (London:

George Allen & Unwin, Ltd., 1950), pp. 530–534.

60. Fackre, *Do and Tell*, p. 15.

61. J. C. Hoekendijk, *Church*, pp. 25–26; H. Hoekendijk, *Horizons*, pp. 22–35; cf. Hans J. Margull, *Hope in Action* (Muhlenberg Press, 1962), pp. 38–69; *Evangelism for a New Day: Building and Renewing Christian Community* (United Church Board for Homeland Ministries, 1972), p. 15.

62. H. Hoekendijk, *Horizons*, p. 30.

63. Jürgen Moltmann, "Existenzgeschichte und Weltgeschichte," *Evangelische Kommentare* (1968), Vol. I, p. 19.

64. Gabriel Fackre, "Evangelism: Meaning, Context Mandate," *The Christian Ministry*, March, 1973, p. i, quoted in "Perspectives on Evangelism," *JSAC Grapevine* (Joint Strategy and Action Committee, New York), V:2 (July 1973), p. 1.

65. *The Church for Others and the Church for the World: A Quest for Structures for Missionary Congregations* (Geneva: World Council of Churches, 1967), pp. 69–71.

66. Shoki Coe, "In Search of Renewal in Theological Education," *Theological Education*, IX:4 (Summer 1973), p. 241.

67. Cox, *Seduction*, p. 174; Moltmann, *Hope*, pp. 180–181.

68. Ahron Sapezian, "Theology of Liberation—Liberation of Theology: Educational Perspectives," *Theological Education*, IX:4 (Summer 1973), p. 259.

69. Freire, *Pedagogy*, pp. 75–76.

70. Sapezian, "Theology of Liberation," *Theological Education*, Summer, 1973; cf. Cone, "Dialectic of Theology and Life."

71. Margull, *Hope in Action*, pp. 59–61.

72. J. C. Hoekendijk, *Church*, pp. 21–24.

73. Lengsfeld, *Überlieferung*, pp. 30–32.

74. Margull, *Hope in Action*, p. 280.

5: INCARNATION AND HUMANIZATION

1. Daly, *Beyond*, p. 11.

2. Juan Luis Segundo, *The Community Called Church*, 5

vols., *A Theology for Artisans of a New Humanity* (Orbis Books, 1973), Vol. I, p. 35.

3. Karl Barth, *The Humanity of God* (John Knox Press, 1970), pp. 37–51.

4. Durham, "Shalom," in Durham and Davies (eds.), *Proclamation,* pp. 280 f.

5. N. W. Porteous, "Man, Nature of, in the OT," *Interpreter's Dictionary,* Vol. III, pp. 242–246; Alves, *Theology,* p. 33.

6. Hahn, *Mission in the New Testament,* pp. 19, 35 f.

7. Porteous, "Man," *Interpreter's Dictionary,* Vol. III, p. 245.

8. Moltmann, *Theology,* p. 104.

9. Oscar Cullmann, *The Christology of the New Testament* (The Westminster Press, 1957), p. 80; Kaufman, "Imago Dei," *Journal of Religion,* July, 1956, p. 160.

10. Günther Bornkamm, *Jesus of Nazareth* (Harper & Brothers, 1960), p. 189.

11. Dorothee Sölle, *Christ the Representative* (Fortress Press, 1967), p. 14.

12. Cullmann, *Christology,* p. 51.

13. Sölle, *Christ,* p. 104.

14. Käsemann, *Jesus Means Freedom,* p. 76; Moltmann, *Gospel,* p. 55.

15. E. C. Blackman, "Incarnation," *Interpreter's Dictionary,* Vol. II, p. 694.

16. Christ and Collins, "Shattering," *Reflection,* March, 1972, pp. 13–14; Rosemary Radford Ruether, "Male Clericalism and the Dread of Women," *The Ecumenist,* XI:5 (July–Aug. 1973), p. 65.

17. Daly, *Beyond,* pp. 79, 96.

18. Norman Perrin, *Rediscovery of the Teaching of Jesus* (Harper & Row, Publishers, Inc., 1967), pp. 224–225; Joseph A. Johnson, "Jesus, the Liberator," in James J. Gardiner and J. Deotis Roberts (eds.), *Quest for a Black Theology* (Pilgrim Press, 1971), p. 105.

19. Sayre, *Are Women Human?* pp. 46–47.

20. Swidler, "Jesus Was a Feminist," *Catholic World,* Jan., 1971, p. 177.

21. *Contra* Daly, who rejects Jesus as a model for women; cf. Daly, *Beyond,* pp. 73–81.

22. Blackman, "Incarnation," *Interpreter's Dictionary,* Vol. II, p. 696.

23. I Cor. 15:47–49; I have translated *Adam, anthrōpos,* and *choïkos* as *human.*

24. Herzog, *Liberation Theology,* p. 265. For a discussion of the scandal of black suffering in relation to "humanocentric theism," cf. W. R. Jones, *Is God a White Racist?* pp. 185–202.

25. Densmore, "On Sisterhood," in Adams and Briscoe (eds.), *Up Against the Wall, Mother,* p. 473.

26. Dumas, "Biblical Anthropology," in *Concerning the Ordination of Women,* p. 30; Trible, "Eve and Adam," *Andover Newton Quarterly,* March, 1973, p. 252.

27. Schoors, *I Am God Your Savior,* pp. 49–50. Quoted by Schoors from V. de Leeuw, *De Ebed Jahweh-Profetiëen* (Assen, 1956), p. 138.

28. Cullmann, *Christology,* pp. 78–79.

29. Johnson, "Jesus, the Liberator," in Gardiner and Roberts (eds.), *Quest,* p. 107; Alves, *Theology,* p. 117.

30. Ferdinand Klostermann, *Das Christliche Apostolat* (Innsbruck, 1962), pp. 108 ff.

31. Hans Küng, *The Church* (Sheed & Ward, Inc., 1967), p. 437.

32. Hans Küng, *Why Priests? A Proposal for a New Church Ministry* (Doubleday & Company, Inc., 1972), pp. 39–40.

33. Daly, *Beyond,* p. 35; cf. Nancy van Vuuren, *The Subversion of Women as Practiced by Churches, Witch-hunters, and Other Sexists* (The Westminster Press, 1973).

34. Freire, *Education,* p. 44; Daly, *Beyond,* p. 36.

35. Karl Barth, *Church Dogmatics: A Selection,* ed. by G. W. Bromiley (Harper & Row, Publishers, Inc., 1961), p. 228.

36. Jürgen Moltmann, "Hope and the Biomedical Future of Man," in Ewert H. Cousins (ed.), *Hope and the Future of Man* (Fortress Press, 1972), p. 98.

37. Bührig, in Preston (ed.), *Technology and Social Justice,* p. 304.

38. Cox, *Seduction,* p. 232.

39. LaVonne Althouse, "Feminism as Enlightenment," *Point of View*, III:3 (Feb. 1973; Metropolitan Christian Council of Philadelphia, 1520 Race Street, Philadelphia, Pa. 19102), pp. 2–3.

40. David Martin, "The Status of the Human Person in the Behavioral Sciences," in Preston (ed.), *Technology and Social Justice*, p. 255.

41. Margaret Mead, *Male and Female* (Dell Publishing Company, 1949), pp. 114–115.

42. Cyril Richardson, "Matristics and Patristics" (Unpublished lecture at Union Theological Seminary, New York City, Oct. 31, 1973).

43. Sayre, *Are Women Human?* p. 37.

44. *Ibid.*, p. 33.

45. C. Richardson, "Matristics and Patristics."

46. B. and T. Roszak (eds.), *Masculine/Feminine*, pp. vii–xi; Daly, *Beyond*, p. 15.

47. Dixon, "Why Women's Liberation?" in Adams and Briscoe (eds.), *Up Against the Wall, Mother*, p. 426.

48. Hannah Arendt, *The Human Condition* (The University of Chicago Press, 1958), pp. 7–11, quoted in Pamela Kearon and Barbara Mehrof, "Prostitution," in Koedt and Firestone (eds.), *Notes from the Third Year: Women's Liberation*, p. 71.

49. Derrick Sherwin Bailey, *Sexual Relation in Christian Thought* (Harper & Brothers, 1959), pp. 291–212; Daly, *Beyond*, p. 105; George H. Tavard, *Woman in Christian Tradition* (University of Notre Dame Press, 1973), pp. 227f.

50. Mitchell, "The Longest Revolution," in B. and T. Roszak (eds.), *Masculine/Feminine*, p. 166; Suzanne Keller, "The Future Role of Women," *The Annals of the American Academy of Political and Social Science*, Vol. 408 (July 1973), pp. 1–12.

51. Dodd H. Bogart and Havens C. Tipps, "The Threat from Species O," *The Futurist*, VII:2 (April 1973), pp. 63–65; Carl E. Braaten, "Untimely Reflections on Women's Liberation," *Dialog* 10 (Spring 1971), p. 105.

52. Russell, *Ferment*, pp. 42–48.

53. Thomas F. Green, *Work, Leisure and the American*

Schools (Random House, Inc., 1968), pp. 76–114.

54. Violette Lindbeck, "A Theological Analysis of Women's Liberation Movements," *Reflection* (Yale Divinity School), LXIX:4 (May 1972), p. 7; Keller, "Future Role of Women," *The Annals of the American Academy of Political and Social Science,* July, 1973, pp. 4–5.

55. "Volunteer Beware!" (NOW Task Force: Women and Volunteerism, P.O. Box 7024, Berkeley, Calif. 94707).

56. Dixon, "Why Women's Liberation?" in Adams and Briscoe (eds.), *Up Against the Wall, Mother,* p. 421.

57. Robert T. Francoeur, "Morality and the New Embryology," *IDOC,* 15 (Aug. 1970), p. 93; cf. Robert T. Francoeur, *Eve's New Rib* (Harcourt Brace Jovanovich, 1972); Herbert Otto, "Man-Woman Relationships in the Society of the Future," *The Futurist,* VII:2 (April 1973), pp. 55–61.

58. Herbert W. Richardson, *Nun, Witch, Playmate: The Americanization of Sex* (Harper & Row, Publishers, Inc., 1971), pp. 1–22.

59. Cox, *Seduction,* p. 236.

60. J. G. Davies, *Every-Day God* (London: SCM Press, Ltd., 1973), "The Holy in Sexual Relations," pp. 158–172.

61. This phrase seems to have originated with Corrie M. Van Asch Van Wijk, past president of the World YWCA.

62. Bailey, *Sexual Relation,* p. 296.

63. Alice Rossi, "Sex Equality: The Beginning of Ideology," in B. and T. Roszak (eds.), *Masculine/Feminine,* pp. 179–186; Daly, *Beyond,* pp. 99–100; Mount, *Feminine Factor,* pp. 48–49.

64. Rossi, "Sex Equality," in B. and T. Roszak (eds.), *Masculine/Feminine,* pp. 184–185.

65. Bailey, *Sexual Relation,* pp. 283–284.

6: Communion in Dialogue

1. *The Church for Others,* p. 19; Moltmann, *Gospel,* pp. 78–94.

2. Thomas O'Meara, "Theologies and Liberations," *LINK,* April 16, 1973, (P.Q. Box, Kansas City, Mo. 64141).

3. Arndt and Gingrich (eds.), *A Greek-English Lexicon of the New Testament.*

4. Freire, *Pedagogy,* p. 76.

5. *The Church for Others,* p. 92; Joseph Ratzinger, *The Open Circle* (Sheed & Ward, Inc., 1966); Michael Novak, *The Open Church* (The Macmillan Company, 1963). In this chapter and elsewhere I am following current usage in distinguishing in *ecclesiology* between *ecclesial* (theological perspective on the church) and *ecclesiastical* (church organization).

6. Colin Williams, *New Directions in Theology Today,* Vol. IV: *The Church* (The Westminster Press, 1968), p. 19.

7. "Mission in God's Mission," in Thomas Wieser (ed.), *Planning for Mission* (U.S. Conference for the World Council of Churches, 1966), p. 49; *The Church for Others,* pp. 69–71.

8. *The Church for Others,* p. 12.

9. Wolfgang Schrage, "Ekklesia und Synagoge," *Zeitschrift für Theologie und Kirche,* LX (1963), pp. 178–202.

10. Adolf Harnack, *Mission and Expansion of the Church in the First Three Centuries* (Harper Torchbook, 1961), pp. 87 ff.

11. Karl Barth, *Church Dogmatics,* ed. by G. W. Bromiley and T. F. Torrance, tr. by G. W. Bromiley (Edinburgh: T. & T. Clark, 1962), Vol. IV, Pt. 3, p. 796; cf. Dieter Manecke, *Mission als Zeugendienst* (Published dissertation, Wuppertal: Brockhaus, 1972).

12. This term is used in the WCC study of "Dialogue with People of Living Faiths and Ideologies," a subunit of Faith and Witness; cf. S. J. Samartha, "Dialogue as a Continuing Concern of Christians," *The Ecumenical Review,* April, 1971, pp. 129–142; cf. S. J. Samartha (ed.), *Dialogue Between Men of Living Faiths,* papers presented at a Consultation held at Ajaltoun Lebanon, March 1970 (Geneva: World Council of Churches, 1971).

13. Owen C. Thomas (ed.), *Attitudes Toward Other Religions* (Harper & Row, Publishers, Inc., 1969), "Introduction," p. 7; cf. Carl F. Hallencreutz, *New Approaches to Men*

of Other Faiths (Geneva: World Council of Churches, 1970).

14. Hans Küng, "The Freedom of Religions," in Thomas (ed.), *Attitudes*, p. 199.

15. *Ibid.*, p. 211; Heinz Robert Schlette, *Towards a Theology of Religions* (Herder & Herder, Inc., 1966), p. 81.

16. Gutiérrez, *Theology of Liberation*, p. 260; "Dogmatic Constitution on the Church" *(Lumen Gentium)*, Abbott (ed.), *Documents of Vatican II*, p. 26, par. 9; Yves Congar, *The Wide World My Parish* (Helicon Press, Inc., 1961), pp. 98–134; cf. E. Hillman, *Wider Ecumenism* (London: Burns & Oates, Ltd., 1968).

17. Abbott (ed.), *Documents of Vatican II*, pp. 30–35, pars. 13–16.

18. *Lumen Gentium*, Abbott (ed.), *Documents of Vatican II*, p. 78, par. 18.

19. Ratzinger, *Open Circle*, pp. 109–116; Ratzinger is quoting from Karl Barth, *Church Dogmatics*, ed. by G. W. Bromiley and T. F. Torrance, tr. by G. W. Bromiley and others (Edinburgh: T. & T. Clark, 1957), Vol. II, Pt. 2, pp. 171, 187, 196.

20. Küng, "Freedom of Religions," in Thomas (ed.), *Attitudes*, p. 216.

21. Moltmann, *Theology*, pp. 304–338; cf. Daly, *Beyond*, pp. 157–169. Daly speaks of the women's revolution as an exodus community.

22. Ruether, *Liberation*, pp. 154–155.

23. Cox, *Seduction*, p. 249.

24. Lawrence Howard, quoted by Maguire, "The Necessity of Thinking Black."

25. Samartha, "Dialogue," *The Ecumenical Review*, April, 1971, p. 135, cf. B. R. Voss, *Der Dialog in der frühchristlichen Literatur* (Munich: W. Fink, 1970).

26. Paul Tillich, "Dialogue," in Thomas (ed.), *Attitudes*, p. 180; Robert McAfee Brown, *The Ecumenical Revolution* (Doubleday & Company Inc., Anchor Book, 1969), pp. 70–79; *Nostra Aetate*, Abbott (ed.), *Documents of Vatican II*, pp. 660–668; Gérard Vallée, "The Word of God and the Living Faiths of Other Men; Chronology of a Study-Process," *Study Encounter*, VI:4 (1970), pp. 1–8; Max Warren, "Presence and Proclamation," in McGavran (ed.), *Eye of the Storm*, p. 202.

27. "Dialogue Between Christians and Marxists," *Study Encounter,* IV:1 (1968), entire issue.

28. Jan Lochmann, "Marxist-Christian Dialogue" (Unpublished speech delivered at Union Theological Seminary, New York City, November, 1968).

29. Samartha, "Dialogue," *The Ecumenical Review,* April, 1971, pp. 135–136.

30. Ruether, "Sexism," *The Christian Century,* Dec. 12, 1973, pp. 1228–1229. For the problems of incommunication between oppressors and oppressed, cf. *Risk,* IX:2 (1973). The entire issue on A Symposium on Black Theology and Latin American Theology is entitled "Incommunication."

31. J. Deotis Roberts, *Liberation and Reconciliation,* Ch. II, "Liberation and Reconciliation," pp. 26–48.

32. Freire, *Pedagogy,* p. 40.

33. *Ibid.,* pp. 41–42; Firestone, *Dialectic of Sex,* pp. 205–242.

34. Cone, "Black Theology and Reconciliation," *Christianity and Crisis,* Jan. 22, 1973, p. 308.

35. Roberts, *Liberation and Reconciliation,* p. 28.

36. Ruether, *Liberation,* p. 169; cf. John A. Morsell, "Ethnic Relations of the Future," *The Annals of the American Academy of Political and Social Science,* Vol. 408 (July 1973), pp. 83–93.

37. Jeanne Richie, "Church, Caste and Women," in Martin E. Marty and Dean G. Peerman (eds.), *New Theology,* No. 8 (The Macmillan Company, 1971), p. 261.

38. Peter L. Kranz, "The Struggles of a Middle-Class White Within a Racial Confrontation Group," *Journal of Intergroup Relations,* Feb., 1972.

39. Freire, *Pedagogy,* pp. 48–49; Van Vuuren, *Subversion of Women,* pp. 164–168.

40. Rosemary Radford Ruether, "The Cult of True Womanhood," *Commonweal,* XCIX:6 (Nov. 9, 1973), p. 132.

41. Phyllis Chesler, "Are We a Threat to Each Other?" *Ms.,* I:4 (Oct. 1972), pp. 88–89; cf. Phyllis Chesler, *Woman and Madness* (Doubleday & Company, Inc., 1972); Dixon, "Why Women's Liberation?" in Adams and Briscoe (eds.), *Up Against the Wall, Mother,* p. 423.

42. Daly, *Beyond,* p. 51.

43. Philip G. Zimbardo and others, "A Pirandellian Prison," *The New York Times Magazine*, April 8, 1973, pp. 38–53, 56–60; Firestone, *Dialectic of Sex*, p. 138; Franz Fanon, *Toward the African Revolution* (Grove Press, Inc., 1967), pp. 99–105.

44. Mount, *Feminine Factor*, p. 178.

45. Doely (ed.), *Women's Liberation*, Appendix I, p. 99.

46. Ruether, "Male Clericalism," *The Ecumenist*, July-Aug. 1973, p. 68.

47. Alice Hageman (ed.), *Sexist Religion and Women in the Church: No More Silence* (Association Press, 1974). Some of the material in Chapters V and VI appears in my article published in this collection; cf. Florence V. Bryant, "Church Employed Women: Economy Class Citizens," *A.D.*, Nov., 1973, pp. 19–23.

48. Richie, "Church," in Marty and Peerman (eds.), *New Theology* No. 8, pp. 259–260; Gregory Baum, "Ministry in the Church," *The Ecumenist*, XI:5 (July–Aug. 1973), p. 78.

49. Küng, *The Church;* Küng, *Why Priests?;* H. Richard Niebuhr, Daniel Day Williams, and James Gustafson, *The Advancement of Theological Education* (Harper & Brothers, 1957); Charles R. Fielding, *Education and Ministry* (Dayton: American Association of Theological Schools, 1966); "Theological Curriculum for the 1970's," *Theological Education*, IV:3 (Spring 1968), pp. 668–734; Stephen G. Mackie, *Patterns of Ministry* (London: William Collins Sons & Co., Ltd., 1969).

50. Russell, "Tradition as Mission," p. 263.

51. Anthony T. Hanson, *The Pioneer Ministry* (London: SCM Press, 1969), pp. 85–87; Küng, *The Church*, p. 383; *Lumen Gentium*, Abbott (ed.), *Documents of Vatican II*, pp. 26–27, par. 10.

52. H. Richard Niebuhr and Daniel Day Williams (eds.), *The Ministry in Historical Perspective* (Harper & Brothers, 1956), pp. 19, 213; Küng, *The Church*, pp. 402, 404–405.

53. C. Richardson, "Matristics and Patristics."

54. Charlotte von Kirschbaum, "Der Dienst der Frau in der Wortverkündigung," *Theologische Studien*, 31 (Zurich: Evangelischer Verlag, Zollikon, 1951), pp. 5–13; Edward B. Fiske, "Anglicans and Catholics Reach Accord on Ministry," *The New York Times*, Dec. 13, 1973, pp. 1, 58.

55. C. Richardson, "Matristics and Patristics."

56. George H. Williams, "The Ministry in the Ante-Nicene Church" (ca. 125–325), H. R. Niebuhr and D. D. Williams (eds.), *Ministry*, pp. 27–30.

57. Joseph Fichter, "The Myth of the Hyphenated Clergy," *The Critic*, XXVIII:3 (Dec. 1968–Jan., 1969), pp. 16–24.

58. Lewis S. Mudge (ed.), *Model for Ministry* (The United Presbyterian Church U.S.A., 1970); *Work Book for the Assembly Committees*, Uppsala, 1968 (Geneva: World Council of Churches, 1968), "Patterns of Ministry," p. 128; T. W. Manson, *The Church's Ministry* (London: Hodder & Stoughton, Ltd., 1948), p. 81; C. Williams, *The Church*, p. 127.

59. Margaret Sittler Ermath, *Adam's Fractured Rib* (Fortress Press, 1970).

60. Emily Hewitt and Susan Hiatt, *Women Priests, Yes or No?* (The Seabury Press, Inc., 1973); S. Ethne Kennedy (ed.), *Women in Ministry* (Chicago: National Assembly of Women Religious, 1972), p. 34.

61. Kennedy (ed.), *Women in Ministry;* Sara Butler, "Sisters in Liturgical Ministry," *Liturgy*, XVIII:10 (Dec. 1973), pp. 15–20; Mary Lynch, "The Deaconess Movement," *Liturgy*, Dec., 1973, pp. 28–29.

62. Daly, "The Courage to See," *The Christian Century*, Sept. 22, 1971, pp. 1108–1111.

63. Roland Bainton, "The Ministry in the Middle Ages," H. R. Niebuhr and D. D. Williams (eds.), *Ministry*, pp. 82–89.

64. Wilhelm Pauck, "The Ministry in the Time of the Continental Reformation," H. R. Niebuhr and D. D. Williams (eds.), *Ministry*, p. 112.

65. Fielding, *Education and Ministry;* H. Richard Niebuhr and others, *The Purpose of the Church and Its Ministry* (Harper & Brothers, 1956); "Theological Curriculum for the 1970's," *Theological Education*, Spring, 1968, pp. 668–734.

66. Oliveira and Calame, *IDAC 3* (1973), 4; David Reed and Luis Ruiz, "Political Education, An Experience in Peru," *IDAC 4* (1973), p. 1.

67. Letty M. Russell, *Christian Education in Mission* (The Westminster Press, 1967), p. 52.

68. "Ordination: A Questionable Goal for Women," *The Ecumenist*, XI:5 (July–Aug. 1973), p. 84.